DEAR PAUL

DEAR PAUL

by

Wesley Harris

Salvation Books
The Salvation Army International Headquarters
London, United Kingdom

First published 2008

ISBN 978 0 85412 787 0

Cover design by Nathan Sigauke

Published by Salvation Books
The Salvation Army International Headquarters
101 Queen Victoria Street, London EC4V 4EH, United Kingdom

Printed by UK Territory Print & Design Unit

Contents

Introduction

I RARELY remember any details of the dreams I have. However, one morning, with a laugh, I told my wife I could remember a particularly vivid and rather ridiculous dream in which I was writing to the Apostle Paul. She said, 'Why don't you do it?' Writing an epistle to an apostle long departed from this life was not something I had contemplated but I sat down and typed some imaginary letters to Paul and sent them to Major Charles King, then the editor of *Salvationist,* a weekly magazine published by The Salvation Army in the United Kingdom.

The letters were published as a series which ran over 20 months. They covered a variety of topics as they occurred to me, not in any particular sequence. With the prospect of them being gathered into a book I later put the letters into groups according to their main subject matter and added Scripture references (from the *New International Version*, except where otherwise stated) for the benefit of anyone wishing to use the letters for Bible study or daily devotional readings.

Sadly, I have never received a reply from the Apostle Paul but I hope that sharing the letters through this book will encourage others to explore the life and letters of the great apostle and discover more of God's will for their lives.

Wesley Harris
Commissioner
Melbourne, Australia
May 2008

1: A letter of introduction

Dear Paul,

I HOPE you won't object to me addressing you as 'Paul'. Nowadays it's fashionable to use first names even when addressing strangers, although I'm not always comfortable with that myself. I thought of beginning, 'Dear Saint ...' but felt that might embarrass you. I recall you once called yourself 'the chief of sinners'.[1] That seems a bit over the top to me, but it was obviously how you felt about yourself when you wrote your epistles 2,000 years ago.

It may surprise you that many of your letters are still being read two millennia later. I get the impression you dashed some of them off in a hurry to meet particular situations, and probably thought they would end up on a bonfire pretty soon after being read just the once.

But you must be pleased, as well as amazed, that millions of us, living in a world very different from the one you knew, find your words timely because they are timeless. We are surrounded by gadgetry that blows the mind. We can speak to people on the other side of the world and even see them on screens. And would you believe some brave souls have even flown to the moon?

But although people have triumphed over outer space they still have problems with 'inner space' – what you called 'the flesh'. People still need to be saved from themselves, which is why the good news you preached is as up-to-date as today's newspaper – or the latest papyrus from Rome was in your day.

You told young Timothy that the Scriptures are inspired or 'God-breathed'[2] and we Christians now believe it's the same with your writings. You must find that awesome! However, a few things seem unclear. In some cases we may have got hold of the wrong end of the stick. That can easily happen when, instead of personal contact, people have to rely on letters, especially, as in this instance, those written in a different age.

I'd like to drop you a line on a few of these points, if only to clear my own mind. I'll keep what I have to say short, because long letters can be tiresome, even for someone with eternity at their disposal.

I've never written to an apostle before, and I can't find anyone with previous experience to guide me on the appropriate approach. So forgive me if I put a foot (I mean a pen) wrong. Expect to hear more from me shortly.

Yours respectfully,

Wesley

1 Timothy 1:15 (KJV); *2 Timothy 3:16*

2: A letter about family

Dear Paul,

I HOPE this isn't too personal, but I've been wondering about your family. Not much is known, so I have to make a few assumptions, which could be risky. Forgive me if I go wide of the mark. Did your family cut you off when you became a Christian? That happened to a Jewish Christian friend of mine. It hurt him terribly and I thought that perhaps family support was one of the things you had to count as a loss in order to gain Christ.

I wonder if there was a rift with your relatives when you returned home to Tarsus after your conversion. At least one member of your family was still ready to help you out of a difficult situation when there was a plot to assassinate you.[1] Did your sister and her family live in Jerusalem, I wonder – and were you able to keep in touch?

It's likely that your father belonged to the Pharisaic guild, said by the historian Josephus to have numbered about 6,000. I take it you were born into it[2] and brought up with very strict observance of the Jewish law and tradition. You appear to have spent formative years at Tarsus[3] in a country we now call Turkey. It was a university city, so you would have been exposed to the world of Greek culture. That would certainly have helped when you became an apostle to the Gentiles – that and your ability with languages.

I imagine your family was wealthy, as they could afford to send you away for further education under Professor Gamaliel.[4] Might they have been involved in the business of weaving tent cloth out of the hair of goats from herds which grazed on the Taurus mountains? Wasn't that a local industry? You were a tent maker yourself, as apparently it was the rule for orthodox Jewish sons to learn a trade, whatever their financial prospects or academic aspirations.

You said you were born a Roman citizen[5] and there are a number of suggestions about how that came about. I believe that sometimes citizenship was given to the population of a whole town or area as a mark of appreciation, but however citizenship came your way it certainly provided you with a number of privileges. For example, although you spoke of being spiritually crucified with Christ, actual physical crucifixion would have been a 'no-no' for a citizen of Rome. Forty or so years before you were born, the celebrated meeting of Cleopatra and Mark Anthony took place at Tarsus and I wonder if older members of your family sometimes recalled that event in their table talk.

I am intrigued by a reference to Andronicus and Junius as 'my relatives who have been in prison with me'.[6] You said that they were Christians before you were. Writing to the Romans you also revealed something of your agony of heart over the wider circle of your 'kinspeople', the Jews who were as yet unsaved. I can well understand how you felt about people you loved who did not love your Lord. To Jewish people family life has always been important and no doubt you had a keen concern for those who, for all their zeal for the law, did not accept the Saviour. But on your knees you glimpsed the vast, extended family which was yours – and ours – in Christ. You wrote, 'For this reason I kneel before the Father, from whom the whole family in heaven and on earth derives its name'.[7]

Yours gratefully,

Wesley

[1]*Acts 23:16;* [2]*Philippians 3:5;* [3]*Acts 21:39;* [4]*Acts 22:3;* [5]*Acts 22:28;* [6]*Romans 16:7;* [7]*Ephesians 3:14, 15*

5

3: A letter about student days

Dear Paul,

I WONDER how you feel as you look back on your days as a student. Did you travel from Tarsus for further studies in Jewish literature and law in Jerusalem? That would have been a new experience for you although it seems you previously spent some of your childhood there.[1] Is that how it was? I remember my heart beating faster when I caught my first glimpse of 'the holy city' so I'm sure yours always did the same.

Coming from a provincial city to pursue studies you might well have found Jerusalem a bit scary at first. Then your pulse would have quickened as every day you 'walked on pages of history', the very stones of the old city reminding you of the great people of your nation's past. It would have been exciting in the narrow streets to rub shoulders with pilgrims from many countries and study with young men from religious traditions similar to your own but from very different backgrounds.

We don't know how long you were engaged in those studies or the precise date of them. Was your sister living in the city at the time and did you stay with her? Did that comfort your elderly parents, thinking of you so far away from home? It's been suggested you might have attended the 'Synagogue of the Freedmen'[2] which presumably was a place of worship favoured by people from your home city or district of Cilicia. That could have brought support from people who knew your family.

Clearly, you took pride[3] in the fact that you studied under the legendary 'professor' Gamaliel who held the honoured title of

Rabban. Apparently, he was of a relatively liberal school of thought and opposed rigorous action against the Apostles when they were brought before the Sanhedrin. Did something of his open-heartedness affect your later attitudes? In the meantime, did your zealous spirit react against the moderate thinking of your teacher and make you all the more determined to root out, and perhaps even kill, members of the Christian sect?

I wonder, did you ever set eyes on Jesus in the flesh? Some believe you did, but many feel you did not or you would have been sure to mention it specifically somewhere in your letters. Anyway, if you ever did catch sight of the Teacher from Nazareth did your prejudice prevent you from seeing him for what he really was? Or deep within you was there a reaction you didn't want to recognise – a pricking of conscience against which your subconscious mind kicked hard?

I don't know and my guesses might be wide of the mark. Much later you wrote to your friends at Corinth: 'So from now on we regard no-one from a worldly point of view. Though we once regarded Christ in this way, we do so no longer.'³ On the road to Damascus you *really* encountered Christ as Lord and were never the same again. Right? Your testimony was, 'If anyone is in Christ, he is a new creation; the old has gone, the new has come!'⁴

For you, as for many people, student days may have been stimulating, enriching, perplexing and enjoyable. I wish I knew more about the influences playing on your mind in those formative years. Without doubt God used them to help make you the man he wanted you to be.

Yours sincerely,

Wesley

¹*Acts 22:3;* ²*Acts 6:9;* ³*Acts 22:3;* ⁴*2 Corinthians 5:16, 17*

4: A letter about sport

Dear Paul,

SPORT is a great thing these days. For many people it's a diversion but for some it's an obsession or even a substitute religion. I gather it wasn't very different in your day. I have read that the Olympic Games attracted great interest, having evolved from contests in honour of some god, or dead hero. After your time, the Games lost their popularity because of cheating. Now they have been revived but because human nature hasn't changed much we still have problems with cheats who take drugs to enhance their performance.

I understand that most great cities in your time had their sporting events and I guess Tarsus was no exception. Although it might have been against orders and regulations for junior Jews, I wonder whether as a lad you nipped along to the local arena to have a peep at what was going on. No disrespect, but I wouldn't be surprised!

Certainly, I pick up from your letters that you had more than a little admiration for the dedication and discipline many athletes brought to their sport. I'm afraid that is in marked contrast to the casual, half-hearted approach which some Christians nowadays bring to the practice of their faith.

You will recall writing along those lines in your first letter to the church in Corinth, the city near which the famous Isthmian Games were held every two years. They featured 'leaping', discus throwing, racing, boxing and wrestling. You wrote: 'Everyone who competes in the games goes into strict training. They do it to get a crown that will not last; but we do it to get a crown that will last for ever.'[1]

8

You went on to say that you made your body your slave or 'kept it under' lest, having preached to others, you might become disqualified yourself. If you, with all your experience, recognised the danger of dropping out, how much more the rest of us need to be 'strong in the grace of the Lord'!

In your second letter to young Timothy your words were: 'If anyone competes as an athlete, he does not receive the victor's crown unless he competes according to the rules.'[2] I agree that there is a world of difference between a group of kids kicking a ball about and teams playing at the highest level. And there is little comparison between the casual jogger and the one who concentrates a lifetime on achieving excellence in a chosen contest.

I don't want to embarrass you, but one of the things which makes you one of my heroes is that you never settled for spiritual mediocrity but maintained your pursuit of excellence to the end. You gave your personal testimony when you wrote to the Christians at Philippi: 'I press on towards the goal to win the prize to which God has called me heavenwards in Christ Jesus.'[3]

Between ourselves, I sometimes get a bit out of breath nowadays, but I believe I can find my second wind – the wind of the Spirit – and make it to the finishing tape.

Yours still striving,

Wesley

[1] *1 Corinthians 9:25;* [2] *2 Timothy 2:5;* [3] *Philippians 3:14*

5: A letter about conversion

Dear Paul,

YOU could never have guessed that yours would become the most famous conversion story in history. Nowadays people unconsciously doff their cap to you when they describe a life-changing event as a 'Damascus Road experience'.

Of course, that blinding moment when the risen Christ confronted you on the road was very special. I'm sure you spoke about it often when you gave your personal testimony. But did the process of conversion begin some time earlier when you minded the clothes of those who stoned Stephen, the first Christian martyr? Did something get to you as you heard that man within a stone's-throw of Heaven cry, 'Lord, do not hold this sin against them.'?[1] Did that begin to crack your bigotry and prejudice?

In all sorts of ways God had been preparing you for a special mission but only time and the Holy Spirit would reveal all that involved. However, the Lord gave a preview to Ananias in Damascus. He was scared stiff of meeting you because of your fearsome reputation as a baiter of Christians but the Lord told him, 'This man is my chosen instrument to carry my name before the Gentiles...'.[2] That encouraged him to seek you out although he must have been shaking in his shoes. I'm sure, as you had been struck blind, you would have been glad to see him, in more ways than one!

I wish I could hear you tell more about your emotions at that stage. No doubt you felt the need for time and space in which to sort yourself out. After all, you had experienced a complete U-turn in your life. You thought you were doing God's will before you set out for Damascus but then God pointed you in a completely different direction. Later you said, 'If anyone is in Christ he is a new creation.'[3]

That certainly rang true as far as your own life was concerned. So much about you was changed and yet you were still *you!* I mean, you didn't turn into a carbon copy of Peter or John. There was no way in which you lost your individuality and became a spiritual clone. You retained your characteristic drive and keenness of intellect and I'm glad about that. However, your powers found a new outlet and your life was lifted to a new plane in Christ. I can almost hear you say, 'Hallelujah!' in response to that statement.

During your ministry you were not afraid of debate and discussion about the Christian faith. With some people it would have been heavy going, I guess. But the man with an experience is never at the mercy of the man with an argument. You knew Christ had changed your life. You might agree that your own experience was the most powerful weapon in your armoury. On the way to Damascus you found your destiny and helped many of us to find ours too. I will be eternally glad about that.

Yours sincerely,

Wesley

[1]*Acts 7:60;* [2]*Acts 9:15;* [3]*2 Corinthians 5:17*

6: A letter about the need for quietness

Dear Paul

AT the risk of being impertinent, may I say you don't come across as a silent type? On the contrary, you seem to have an inexhaustible flow of language to use for furtherance of the gospel. Debate and discussion were meat and drink for you. You were a man of *words* for sure. You were also a man of *your* word and a man of *the* Word.

But from youth you would have been taught that there was a time to speak and also a time to be silent. In one version of your correspondence with Christians at Thessalonica you said they should 'study to be quiet'[1] and I think there were times when you too felt the need to take time out for quiet reflection. Is that right? After all, no one could keep giving out as you did without also taking in. As the psalmist puts it, we need to 'Be still and know ....[2]

When you wrote to Christians in Galatia you appeared to give a glimpse of a time when you found this to be especially important.[3] You hadn't been converted long and you had been through a somewhat testing time in the city of Damascus. Did you feel the need for a break, time to sort yourself out and pray through the implications of what had happened to you?

I think that may have been so, and apparently you didn't have consultation with the leaders of the Church just then but went on your own into Arabia instead. Exactly how far you went or how long you stayed we don't know but that large area (then under King Aretas) included some very inhospitable country, as I know from having travelled in that part of the world. It would be interesting to know how you managed for food and shelter. No doubt creature comforts were of little concern; you were more interested in holy days than holidays.

Did you think of Elijah in the wilderness or the similar experience of our Lord? I guess you did. And was it during those days communing with God, away from the hurly burly of life, that you received the inspiration which illumined the subsequent years of your ministry? Was it then you got it all together? Upon the hard anvil of experience did you then hammer out the message you later shared with others? Many have discovered that what appears to be a desert experience can be very fruitful.

I don't think you were a hermit by inclination; rather you were a 'people person' who loved to engage life in all its richness. But in Arabia, and probably many other places as well, I think you may have found in prayer and meditation the secret of recharging depleted spiritual energies. Was it that which helped you avoid what is now known as 'burn out'?

In the country where I live and the part of the Church to which I belong, people are taking part in 'silent retreats'. Some of the more boisterous have wondered how they would cope with hour upon hour of silence. The 'chattering classes' – to which we all belong at times – can find quietness hard to handle. For some it is a new thing, but many testify that it is a beneficial experience.

I think God intended us to have a certain rhythm in life, with a taking in and a giving out, meditation and action, prayer and service. Reading between the lines of your letters I think you feel the same.

Yours hopefully,

Wesley

¹See 1 Thessalonians 4:11 (KJV); ²Psalm 46:10;
³Galatians 1:11-24 (especially v. 17)

7: A letter about suffering and the future

Dear Paul,

I GUESS, from where you are, some of the things which bother us on earth seem of little account. You're able to see everything so clearly now, but I expect you remember writing to your friends at Corinth: 'Now we see but a poor reflection as in a mirror ... Now I know in part.'[1] Well, me too!

I've had a real problem with why people suffer. Of course, our Lord on the Cross cried, 'My God, my God, why?'[2] and at our 'lesser Calvaries' many of us have echoed his words.

The question has particular point when it becomes, 'Why me?' and you know all about that. You had something you called your 'thorn in the flesh'[3] and you would be amazed at how people have tried to guess what it was. Suggestions have included an eye problem, a spinal difficulty and a recurring fever. You may well smile if it was something quite different. Whatever it was, it bothered you and you have told us you prayed repeatedly that God would take it away. In fact, he didn't answer your prayer – at least, not in the way you had in mind. He said, 'My grace is sufficient for you, for my power is made perfect in weakness.'[3] Apparently God could use your disabilities as well as your abilities, and since your time quite a lot of saints have proved that to be true for them.

Sometimes suffering is like a big black cloud and it's difficult to see beyond it. I've been with people as they have watched a loved one dying slowly and painfully and clichés have died on my lips. I've had no easy answer to offer but have simply prayed that my friends might, in faith, stand even when they couldn't understand, believing that for the Christian the best is always yet to be.

You were certainly inspired when you wrote to the Romans: 'I consider that our present sufferings are not worth comparing with the glory that will be revealed in us.'[4] Talk about seeing the rainbow through the rain!

In the same passage you spoke about the whole creation groaning as in the pains of childbirth. Clearly you were conscious of something being fundamentally wrong, a malaise affecting and infecting everything. Fortunately you had the faith to look forward to better things, and you may hardly believe it but the faith of millions of people has been strengthened by your faith. Speaking personally, like most people, I've had my doubts at times, but now I dare to believe that one day I will be with you and countless others, amazed and humbled in the presence of the Lord. That hope kept you going and it helps lots of Christians today.

Yours faithfully,

Wesley

[1] 1 Corinthians 13:12; [2]Matthew 27:46; [3]2 Corinthians 12:7-10; [4]Romans 8:18

8: A letter about the evil I don't want to do

Dear Paul,

WHEN we put pen to paper we never know how far our words will go or what effect they may have. It must be awesome for you to realise that much of what you were inspired to write is now a basis for Christian belief around the world. Apart from our Lord you must be the most quoted person on earth and in many cases it seems that what you wrote arose from your own experience.

For example, when you told the Christians at Corinth that if anyone was in Christ he was a new creation you must have been thinking of that day on the road to Damascus when the Lord arrested you and set your feet in a new direction. I think you never tired of telling people about what was really a pivotal experience in your life. But I'm glad you made clear that the experience of renewal was free for all.

Although Christ brought new direction and victory into your life, would you agree that you still had plenty of battles to fight within yourself as well as with outside forces? Some people imagine that Satan gave you a hard time after your conversion and, for the record, let me say out of *my* experience, that Satan is still doing his dirty work. What you called 'the flesh' is still a challenge. The Christian life is not always easy.

There are things you wrote in what we call the seventh chapter of the letter to the Romans which seem auto-biographical even if you meant us to generalise from them. You

16

wrote: 'For what I do is not the good I want to do; no, the evil I do not want to do – this I keep on doing.'[1]

Did you have in mind your experience before conversion? Or were there later times when, like saints through the ages, you felt you had not measured up to the highest standards and were a disappointment to yourself as well as to the Lord? If that was the case then, in a weird way, I would be encouraged. If I felt you were 'naturally good' and 'perfectly perfect' many of your words might have gone over my head. Your experience would have seemed either too good to be true or at least too good for me. If, in fact, you had to struggle with yourself and then came out on top it could be an encouragement to lesser mortals, especially when you make it clear that your victories were through Christ and the power of the Spirit – resources just as available to us as they were to you.

In a paradoxical way you claimed that what you were was by the grace of God, yet you made clear that Christians (including yourself) had to work out what God had worked in. With a passive receiving of grace there had to be an active striving to be good. You told the Christians at Philippi they should work out their own salvation with fear and trembling, bearing in mind that it was God who was working in them.[2] I can figure that out, and thank you for making it plain.

Yours still trusting and trying,

Wesley

[1]Romans 7:19; [2]Philippians 2:12, 13

17

9: A letter about books and parchments

Dear Paul,

BOOKS have always been important to me. Some are like old friends and I often turn to them for guidance and inspiration. While moving from one country to another in the course of my Christian service a couple of hundred of my volumes were lost and I still mourn over some of them. You will understand that. Books were obviously important to you as well.

I've always used books with paper pages while you had scrolls made of papyrus (manufactured from the pith of plants which grew by rivers) or parchment (made from animal skins). You would have read the work of Greek poets as well as that of Jewish rabbis, and reports about the widespread Roman Empire would have been of interest. But am I right that you especially treasured the Jewish Scriptures and would have felt lost without them?

When you were in prison awaiting execution you wrote to Timothy: 'When you come ... bring my scrolls, especially the parchments.'[1] I wonder about those scrolls. Were they rough drafts of manuscripts you had prepared and were anxious to polish and publish before your life came to an end?

Could they have contained some of the material gathered by your friends Mark and Luke for their accounts of the life of Jesus? They must often have talked with you about their literary efforts and valued your input as a man of letters and a beloved leader. Were you anxious to refresh your memory of some of the stories they had collected? Pondering on the life of our Lord would

18

certainly have lightened your days in prison passing through the 'valley of the shadow of death'.

Then what about the parchments which you were especially anxious to have? Could it be that among them were legal documents, including your certificate of Roman citizenship, which could have been important to you in the circumstances? Or were they portions of the Hebrew Scriptures which had long nourished your soul and could sustain your spirit in testing times?

Doubtless you committed many portions of Scripture to memory or hid them in your heart, as the psalmist put it.[2] But I'm sure you longed to have the written word of the Lord with you.

You may be interested to know that, like you, a friend of my wife's spent a number of years in prison for his faith. He managed to gather scraps of material on which he could write remembered verses of Scripture. Then he passed his 'Bible' to other prisoners eager to share the truth of the gospel. I feel that's the kind of thing you would have done.

I hope the scrolls and parchments reached you.

Yours sincerely,

Wesley

[1]2 Timothy 4:13; [2]Psalm 119:11

10: A letter about being spiritually fit and ageing

Dear Paul,

YOU will be interested to know that many people live longer now than they did in your day, thanks to advances in medical science which would have amazed your friend Dr Luke. But health hazards remain. One in the part of the world where I live is eating too much! People tend to dig their graves with their knives and forks, if you understand what I mean.

Another problem is lack of exercise. Transport has become so easy that many people are slow to do what they were designed to do – walk. I sometimes advise people that they should never ride if it is possible to go on foot but I can't think that lack of exercise would have been a problem for you, except when you were in prison, perhaps. Do you ever think you had too much of a good thing, 'footslogging' from town to town?

I'm sure you had plenty of mental as well as physical exercise. You obviously took very seriously the command to love the Lord with all your mind.[1] The only mental exercise some people get is jumping to conclusions!

However, I picture you, with furrowed brow, thinking your way, step by step, through your intellectual problems. The challenge to think was not one to shirk. But I feel that keeping yourself *spiritually* fit was a priority with you. You told Timothy he should exercise, or train himself, to be godly.[2] You often made it clear that spiritual health, like physical health, is a gift from God, but people have to do their part.

What were the secret disciplines you employed to keep your own soul in peak condition? Did you find it hard going at times? From what you said about evil being present even when you wanted to do good, I think you did.

Reading between the lines again I sense you found it important first to apply to yourself what you preached to others, which is a good exercise for us preachers. You wrote that Christians should pray without ceasing[3] but I would be surprised if you were not sometimes tempted to skip your private prayer sessions when you were tired or preoccupied with problems. You said your people should think about things which were pure but I guess, when you saw the lewdness in a city like Corinth, dark thoughts must sometimes have knocked on the door of your mind, seeking admission.

There can be no discipleship without discipline and I'm sure that, along with prayer, you regarded the study of Scripture as an important exercise which enabled you to keep fit for the Master's use. Regular fellowship with other Christians must also have helped.

When I was young I might have imagined that with the passage of years I would get things worked out and spiritual life would become easier. Now I know that does not automatically happen. Satan never gives up and there are battles to be fought whatever our age or stage may be. But there is grace sufficient so that when we reach what seems like breaking point we need not break.

These are just some of the thoughts which come as a result of reading and re-reading your letters. Thank you again.

Yours sincerely,

Wesley

*[1]Matthew 22:37; Mark 12:30; [2]1 Timothy 4:7;
1 Thessalonians 5:17*

11: A letter about hospitality

Dear Paul,

ON occasion you referred to the gift of hospitality[1] and I guess you had good reason to appreciate its worth. More often than not you wrote of going from 'A' to 'B' without mentioning how you travelled or where you stayed. But this would have been an important part of your life.

Were there times when you could have related to the words of the prophet Isaiah, 'The bed is too short to stretch out on, the blanket too narrow to wrap around you'?[2] And were there occasions when there was no bed at all and you had to lie under the stars with only a stone for a pillow? I'm sure there must have been.

Then I wonder how you managed for food. Were there periods when it was in short supply or when your digestion suffered from local 'delicacies' not to your liking?

I know one of God's travellers who says that when he led evangelistic campaigns around the world he sometimes employed one of the following 'prayers': 'Where he leads me I will follow, what he gives me I will swallow' or 'I'll *get* it down if you'll *keep* it down!'

In my imagination I can picture you with a wry smile as you recollect occasions when you were offered food which was hardly to your taste but which you accepted out of courtesy and consideration for the feelings of your hosts. I have occasionally done the same myself, although more often than not I have greatly enjoyed what has been provided.

You would have had high regard for Christian hospitality for spiritual as well as physical reasons. As you shared an ordinary meal with a family didn't it often become sacramental – not because there was the thought of observing a ritual but because of the memory of the way in which the Lord similarly shared food with his disciples?[3] Hospitality would have provided the occasion when the real presence of Jesus was felt in a wonderful way.

It still can.

I recall occasions when an ordinary meal has become extraordinary because of the same presence. For example, my wife and I visited a country where the government banned many expressions of Christianity for decades. The Church was forced to go underground but as we shared food with dear people who had for years been obliged to remain secret disciples, the joy of Jesus welled within our hearts and we sensed that he was very near to us.

Those who provide hospitality might not have as high a profile in the Church as those who preach or give oversight to congregations but I'm sure you would agree that they also may be hand-servants of the Most High God.

Yours sincerely,

Wesley

[1]Romans 12:13; [2]Isaiah 28:20; [3]Luke 24:30

23

12: A letter about being in prison

Dear Paul,

AS we get older we tend to enter our 'anecdotage'. We like to relive the past and tell anecdotes about 'the olden days'. We may become boring but not necessarily so. For a number of years I have been giving Christian teaching in a state school and, surprisingly, the youngsters say they like to hear about what I have seen of Christian work around the world.

Did you do much talking to children? We know this was a feature of the Lord's ministry[1] but there's little evidence of it with you. That doesn't mean it didn't happen, for the records we have cannot have covered every aspect of your life. There are plenty of gaps to be filled in. Perhaps, when you were working as a tent maker, children gathered to watch and you were able to tell them some of your stories. Was that how it happened?

I'm sure they would have been as fascinated to hear of your experiences as were their elders.

For example, you could have told of the time in Damascus when enemies were out to get you, even setting guards at the city gates in case you slipped away. Some of the houses had windows on the city wall and from one of these, in the dead of night, Christians let you down in a basket at the end of a rope.[2] That was a close shave, and the story would have lost nothing in the telling. You had an even closer call at Lystra when things turned ugly and you were stoned and then left for dead outside the city wall.[3] How badly were you hurt, I wonder? You probably kept a 'stiff upper lip' and didn't let on how you really felt.

24

Another story which would really have made the kids say 'Wow!' would have concerned your shipwreck off Malta.[4] Dr Luke did a marvellous job describing those events in what we call the Acts of the Apostles but you would have been able to add your own personal touches.

I don't know about the children but I for one would like to know more about your secret thoughts and feelings when you were held in Rome for such a long time awaiting trial and a possible death penalty. I have been to Rome and to a traditional site of your imprisonment, although I'm not sure how authentic it was.

For sure, however, you used the time you were in custody to write some wonderful letters. Do you know that after your time a number of other great Christians wrote some of their best works while they were jail birds for Jesus? Their imprisonment too worked out for the furtherance of the gospel, which shows that God can turn even bad experiences to good account.

I think it takes dull people to make Christian ministry dull. It is what we make it, led by the Lord. Certainly, your life was anything but boring. It may have been tough at times but it was most rewarding. Looking back on my own less epic life I would say that for me too it has been thrilling – and still is!

Yours sincerely,

Wesley

[1]*Mark 10:14;* [2]*Acts 9:25;* [3]*Acts 14:19;* [4]*Acts 27:27-43*

13: A letter about humour and holy joy

Dear Paul,

AS I read your letters you emerge from the mists of the past as a very 'knowable' person. Part of your appeal lies in the fact that many of us feel we can identify with you. While you were blessed with very special gifts you were nevertheless bone of our bone and flesh of our flesh. You had a divine message but you were very human.

Inevitably, however, there are gaps in our knowledge of you as a person. I wonder, for example, about your sense of humour. When friends visited you during your house arrest in Rome did you regale them with stories of humorous incidents experienced in the course of your travels – beginning with something like, 'A funny thing happened on the way to ...'? I wouldn't be surprised and I can imagine peals of laughter following your reminiscing. Doubtless, you would have dispensed wit as well as wisdom and I would like to have been a multi-lingual fly on the wall, able to enjoy some of the lighter moments as well as the deeply serious times.

Our Lord employed humour in his teaching. For example, when speaking of people who had big convictions about little things and little convictions about big things, he drew that caricature of the man who strained out a gnat and then swallowed a camel! That may not be your idea of a joke but you did sometimes employ irony, a form of humour.[1] I'm sure there was sometimes a twinkle in your eye and evidence of joy in your heart. I've been reading again your marvellous epistle to the Christians at Philippi. If ever I

26

was prone to drag a heavy heart around like a ball and chain that letter would help me lighten up![2]

I think we need a baptism of holy joy in the Church today. The merchants of gloom and doom are having too much of their own way and your words provide the tonic some of us need.

In your demanding ministry you must have needed a sense of humour to cope with the awkward squads you encountered in some places. I'm sure you were also able to laugh at yourself sometimes. It's said that few people get their heads turned through trying to see the funny side of themselves but you were certainly mature enough to do that on occasion, as we all need to do.

Like pepper and salt, humour makes life more palatable and I can't imagine you not using it. You would agree that the grace of God may be in a good laugh (I don't think we should only baptise earnestness, and regard laughter as pagan. Why should the devil have all the best laughs?). But, as is clear from your writings, joy is much more than good humour although it may well include it, and I'm glad that, like you, I know something of the joy of Jesus.[3] Like you, I too want to share it around.

Joyfully yours,

Wesley

[1] *1 Corinthians 4:8-10;* [2] *Philippians 3:1;* [3] *John 15:11*

14: A letter about physical appearance

Dear Paul,

FOR some people, appearance is all important. They literally make themselves ill with worry if they think their face or their figure is not all it should be. Beauty treatment is now an immense industry, which may or may not be a bad thing. It certainly illustrates the concern people have for their physical image. I guess it was much the same in your day, with Greek athletes and Roman society women being fastidious about how they looked and the impression they made on onlookers. Fashion houses probably catered for the well off then as they do now.

But what about you? Were you concerned about dressing up – or down – to suit the occasion? Were you worried about whether or not artists were keen to paint your portrait? I don't think so. You had other things on your mind. We have no accurate idea of what you looked like, although over the centuries some artists have dipped their brushes into the palette of their imagination and featured you in works of art.

You must have been physically tough to put up with all the hardships which came your way. I also think you were weather-beaten through trudging from place to place on your preaching tours, often under a burning sun. Your hands would have been calloused from working at your trade as a tent maker and you said you bore in your body the marks of the Lord Jesus – possibly a reference to scars from the beatings you endured for the sake of the gospel.[1]

Beyond that, what other educated guesses can we make? Some have thought you had an eye problem, a squint perhaps. I wouldn't want to be offensive, but there were those who felt you weren't as impressive in person as you were in your letters. Whatever anyone thought, I'm sure you would have gone along with the couplet:

My face I don't mind it, for I am behind it –
The people in front feel the jar.

Would you agree that beauty is only skin deep and it's what people are in their hearts and minds which is most important? If you were ever bothered by the poor reflection you saw in a mirror you probably recalled the scriptural statement that, while men and women look on the outward appearance, God looks on the heart.[2]

Of course, physical health and beauty should be appreciated as a gift of God but I think you would have drawn on your knowledge of the psalms and maintained that the most important thing is to worship the Lord in 'the beauty of holiness'.[3] A great saint and leader of the Church who came after your time prayed, 'Lord make me beautiful within' and I feel sure you would add an apostolic Amen to that prayer.

Yours sincerely,

Wesley

[1]*Galatians 6:17; 2 Corinthians 6:5; 11:25;* [2]*1 Samuel 16:7;*
[3]*see Psalm 29:2 (KJV)*

15: A letter about the 'Ephesian Symphony'

Dear Paul,

AS a writer – although not in your league – I'm interested in the way authors tackle their task. Some make numerous drafts while others just pour out the fresh ideas surging in their brains. What about you? I think you sometimes may have paced up and down, hastily pouring out your inspired words while a secretary with scroll in hand tried with difficulty to keep up.[1] But when there was less urgency I think you were inspired to pre-plan a letter and deal systematically with themes suggested by the Holy Spirit.

Your epistle to the church in Rome suggests that, and so does what we call your letter to the Ephesians. It may be fanciful on my part but it reminds me of a great piece of music with various themes being introduced. I have sometimes called it 'The Ephesian Symphony'.

Here are some of the themes I recognise. There's the theme of Christian *worship*.[2] You said: 'I kneel before the Father from whom his whole family in heaven and earth derives its name.'[3] Those words indicate both intimacy and reverence. Did you feel that God was close to you – like a Father – and yet at the same time far above you? It seems to me that in true worship both aspects are important.

You wrote about the Christian's *walk*[4], as some older translations put it, or lifestyle, as we say today. You said we should live up to our calling, or vocation, showing humility, love and patience. What's more, the record shows you not only talked the talk but walked the walk.

You taught about the Christian's *work*[5] in the Church and in the world. You believed in the dignity of labour and worked tirelessly yourself. But you were also aware of what might be called the theology of leisure and the need for proper rest, as indicated in the commandments given to Moses. I confess I've sometimes failed to keep commandments about resting and wonder whether, being an activist, you were been tempted in the same way. I wouldn't be surprised.

Another theme you introduced had to do with the Christian's *war*[6]. You took the powers of evil seriously. Spiritual warfare was more than a figure of speech as far as you were concerned and you urged your fellow Christians to put on the whole armour of God. You said people should take the word of God, which you describe as the 'sword of the Spirit', and also pray on all occasions. That's the only way to gain spiritual victory.

As I tune into your thoughts relayed through Scripture by the power of the Spirit I'm so grateful that you were inspired to write what we now recognise as the word of God to our hearts. The passage of 2,000 years has done nothing to reduce its power or potency, and that's something of a miracle.

Yours gratefully,

Wesley

[1]For instance Galatians 1; [2]Ephesians 1:15ff; [3]Ephesians 3:14; [4]Ephesians 4:1-6; [5]Ephesians 4:11-13; 4:32-5:11; 6:1-4; [6]Ephesians 6:10-l9

16: A letter about anxiety and the peace of God

Dear Paul,

I WOULD like to write to you about something I suspect troubles a lot of Christians: worry. I've noted you sometimes wrote about salvation as something past, sometimes as something to come and at other times as something ongoing. I'm sure, during your lifetime, you were always certain that God was still working on you. Certainly, you never wrote as though you felt that, spiritually speaking, you were the 'finished article'.

In this respect I'm like you. There are layers of my life that still require divine treatment.

One area is to do with anxiety. I don't think I'm an unusually or obsessively anxious person but I confess I do sometimes fret needlessly. I tell people that worry is the interest they pay on tomorrow's troubles, then I waste nervous energy myself bothering about things which may never happen anyway. How silly!

You wrote to the Christians at Philippi: 'Do not be anxious about anything'[1] but I wonder if sometimes you did a bit of worrying yourself. For example, did you worry about that physical disability which you called your 'thorn in the flesh'? Was there a fear that things might go from bad to worse and turn you into an invalid?

Writing to the Corinthians you admitted: 'I face daily the pressure of my concern for all the churches.'[2] Did concern sometimes degenerate into worry? Were there times when even you found it difficult to trust the Lord to overrule and undertake in his own way and time? I wouldn't be surprised if that was so, and in that case you would understand the difficulty some other Christians experience.

You may now have a perspective rather different from when you were 'earthbound'. Where we stand often depends on where we sit! That is, the angle from which we view matters can make all the difference. However, I'm sure you won't forget some of the fears and feelings you had when you trudged the dusty roads of Asia Minor.

You frequently urged people to be accepting of the peace of God – something which was both a gracious gift and a characteristic of the divine character. You said that God's peace, which transcends all understanding, could be like a sentry guarding hearts and minds.[3] You wouldn't have written that unless it had worked for you, and I reckon that a lot of people would like to tap into the secret of your calm confidence and poise.

I had a wise mother-in-law who, when people were becoming unduly troubled, would say, 'It will be all the same in a hundred years from now.' Perhaps we should go a step further and try to see things which bother us in the context of eternity.

Our Lord prescribed an antidote for anxiety. It was that a loving Heavenly Father knew all about his children's needs and would not fail to provide for them.[4] Would you agree that greater peace of mind comes with increased trust in God? I figure that's the way it is but I will pore over your words some more to see what else I can learn on the subject.

Yours still seeking,

Wesley

[1]Philippians 4:6; [2]2 Corinthians 11:28; [3]Philippians 4:7; [4]Matthew 6:8, 25-34

17: A letter about preaching and wisdom

Dear Paul,

IT'S not hard to find subjects to write to you about, because your letters and experiences raise so many points for discussion. You've always struck me as a very focused person. You might not thank me for reminding you, but you were certainly single-minded in your persecution of Christians before your conversion. Mercifully, your focus shifted and your 'magnificent obsession' became the proclamation of the gospel, without which the Early Church would have been decimated.

Speaking personally, in Christian ministry I've sometimes found it difficult to keep the main thing the main thing. Things which are peripheral can easily become central, and the good prove to be the enemy of the best.

Did you ever have this problem, or at least fear you might have lost your essential focus? I wouldn't want to be disrespectful or read too much into your words but I wonder whether you harboured a little self doubt when you wrote to the Christians at Corinth: 'I resolved to know nothing while I was with you except Jesus Christ and him crucified. I came to you in weakness and fear, and with much trembling. My message and my preaching were not with wise and persuasive words.'[1]

I understand you had come from Athens where, seeking to be 'all things to all men', you had tried to meet the philosophers on their own terms.[2] I think that it was a great attempt but, in common with most preachers, did you have the feeling your effort hadn't come off and that the response was not as you wished?

We have only a partial picture of your ministry and many of your activities must be unrecorded but you might not have felt inclined to repeat elsewhere the approach you tried at Athens. At any rate, when you got to Corinth you decided to stick to the simple preaching of Christ crucified. No way would you have had any time for what I have heard described as 'cleveralities'. Your only desire was to communicate the gospel effectively.

In a modest way I've tried to adapt the Christian message to a variety of people and situations but I've sometimes feared I might lose sight of what should be at the very heart of the message, foolish as it may appear to the 'wise' of this world. I could write or speak many things which might help people in one way or another, and that would be fair enough. But the Cross is the plus sign which people need if the message is ultimately to add up as far as they are concerned. You said just that, in better words.

You made it clear that people need more than a philosophy and more than 'self help' – important though that is. We all need a hand from on high, through saving faith in Christ crucified.

You knew that the heart of the human problem is the problem of the human heart and that Jesus is the only Saviour. In the current pluralistic society that kind of claim doesn't always go down well, but you'll be glad to know that many Christians follow your lead.

Yours sincerely,

Wesley

¹1 Corinthians 2:2, 3; ²Acts 17:16-34 especially v. 32

35

18: A letter about pet phrases

Dear Paul,

MANY people who write or speak a great deal have pet phrases which they use repeatedly, almost without realising it. I knew a college principal who had a saying he used so often that his students used to count the number of times it came up in an address!

With respect, Paul, you had such a phrase. If, like me, you had been blessed with a son and daughter they would have you picked up on this point – although I can't imagine that stopping *you* in your tracks. Your special saying occurs in almost all your letters which have survived. It is the phrase, 'in Christ'.

You wrote that you had fathered people in Christ and your way of life was in Christ. You triumphed in Christ and you spoke in Christ.[1] It was a phrase which seemed to come out of the soul and centre of your experience but it was a testimony we all might share, for you said that when *anyone* was in Christ they were a new creation.[2] Obviously, you didn't think of the Church as a 'closed shop' or exclusive society. Allcomers were welcome as far as you were concerned.

Fair enough, you varied the phrase sometimes and spoke of being 'in Christ Jesus' or 'in the Lord'. In your letter to the Romans – in what we now identify as chapter eight – your phrase seems almost interchangeable with 'in the Spirit'.[3] The relationship you had in mind was not physical but spiritual; not dependent on time or space but possessed of an eternal quality. That's why after all these centuries some of us feel we have so much in common with you.

On one occasion you wrote something I found rather odd when I first read it. Your words were: 'Clothe yourselves with the Lord Jesus Christ.'[4] Then I remembered that nowadays if we see a young couple obviously in love we may say, 'Look at them, they're wrapped up in each other', which is a bit like the idea behind your words, don't you think? Through what you would understand as *agape* love we can be wrapped up in Christ. Then there is the complementary thought that we may not only be in Christ but Christ can be in us. That was the gist of the personal testimony you gave to the Galatians: 'Christ lives in me. The life I live in the body, I live by faith in the Son of God who loved me and gave himself for me.'[5] When I read that I want to shout Hallelujah! I'm sure you wouldn't be put off by that.

I find it hard to envisage your present situation for, as you said yourself, it's hard for mere mortals to comprehend what God has prepared for those who love him.[6] But I have a feeling that the life to come is not so much a new life as the one we have lived on earth in Christ carried on under new conditions. As the saying goes, we'll see! In the meantime I enjoy doing my bit to carry on the great work to which you devoted your life. And hopefully, those who have passed on can give a rousing cheer of encouragement. Many through the ages have been helped by that thought.

Yours sincerely,

Wesley

[1] *1 Corinthians 4:15, 17; 2 Corinthians 2:14, 17;*
[2] *2 Corinthians 5:17;* [3] *Romans 8;* [4] *Romans 13:14;*
[5] *Galatians 2:20b;* [6] *1 Corinthians 2:9*

19: A letter about faith and works

Dear Paul,

A STURDY independence seems to have been one of your traits of character. For example, you preferred to earn your living rather than be in anyone else's pocket or dependent on their 'charity'. Yet with regard to the most important things in life you knew you could never be independent, any more than any of us can be.

Salvation was not something you could earn. You tried to do so by a punctilious observance of human rites and the rules and regulations of Judaism. Your zeal knew no bounds but still something was lacking.

Then it hit you between the eyes: what would make the difference was not what you could do but what God had already done in Christ. It was silly to think you could work your passage to Heaven. You had to swallow your pride and, by faith, accept that God in his grace accepted you. You latched on to the words of Habakkuk: 'The righteous will live by his faith'[1], but many people find that difficult. They're put off by the sheer simplicity of the gospel.

This was the problem with some of the Christians you knew in Galatia. They had accepted that salvation was by grace through faith, but then they were led astray and made the mistake of thinking they could settle their account with God by religious observances.[2] Pardon my saying so, but you seem to have got really worked up about this and dashed off a letter which, you may be interested to know, a small group I lead has been studying recently (I guess you never dreamt that any letter of yours would be studied nearly 2,000 years after you wrote it!).

38

What might be called 'Galatianism' is still a problem in some quarters. There are those who think that if they observe certain rituals they will automatically be right with God, which may not necessarily be the case. In fact, as you would agree, there is no grace deemed to be received through rites or rituals which may not be received through faith alone.

Some imagine that by doing good things – like giving to the poor – they can square their account with God and build up credit in Heaven. But if I understand you aright, good works can never be the basis of salvation, although they should be a result of it. If we are saved we will do good things but we will not be saved *by* doing them but by faith in the amazing grace of God revealed in Christ. Right?

However, despite what I have written, I have to confess that I've not always been entirely free from 'Galatianism' myself. I've worked long and hard in Christian service but I have to remind myself that long service will not in itself merit a place for me in Heaven. As Augustus M. Toplady put it:

> *Nothing in my hand I bring,*
> *Simply to thy Cross I cling.*[3]

That's the truth of the matter.

Yours sincerely,

Wesley

[1]Habakkuk 2:4; [2]Galatians 4:9, 10;
Salvation Army Song Book *302 v. 3*

20: A letter about continuing salvation

Dear Paul,

IN the branch of the Church to which I belong it's customary for people to stand up in meetings and testify about what the Lord has done for them. Did you hear testimonies like that in your day? I wouldn't be surprised, for some of your converts must have been almost bursting to speak about the difference it made when they stepped from the darkness of paganism into the light of the gospel. Such testimonies would have warmed your heart as a father in God.

You gave the believers at Corinth a catalogue of the kinds of sinners who could not inherit the Kingdom of God, then you added, in case any of them might forget the pit from which they had been dug, 'That is what some of you were. But you were washed, you were sanctified, you were justified.'[1]

It's marvellous to see salvation working and lives being changed. Nothing has thrilled me more and I guess you would say the same. You wrote to converts in Ephesus: 'By grace you have been saved'[2] and the statement would have reminded them of that special time when they were first converted. Through your words, something of the glow and the glory may have been renewed in their hearts. But did you find that with the passage of years some testimonies became petrified and people spoke of their salvation only in the past tense?

If so, it would explain why you were at pains to point out that salvation was meant to be an ongoing experience. Writing to believers in Corinth you said: 'to us who are being saved it [the Cross] is the power of God'.[3] Am I right in thinking you meant that people should not only know that Jesus had saved them once but that he could save them continually?

As I pore over your letters I notice that you not only thought of salvation as something in the past and present but something in the future as well. Writing to Roman Christians you said: 'Since we have now been justified by his blood how much more shall we be saved?'[4]

Were you thinking of the second coming of the Lord when, in the same letter, you wrote, 'our salvation is nearer now than when we first believed'?[5] Pondering your words, I thought of someone being rescued from a sinking ship. In one sense they could be said to have been saved when they were taken off the stricken vessel; they were being saved when they were in the rescue boat, and they would finally be saved when they reached the shore.

Pardon me if I sound as though I'm trying to teach an apostle! I'm simply trying to get my thoughts around what it means to be saved. Of course, I know what it has meant in my own spiritual experience but I want to understand God's boundless salvation in your terms and take in your God-inspired teaching about it. I rely on the Holy Spirit to help me to understand your words as I read them, even as you relied on him to guide your pen as you wrote.

Yours sincerely,

Wesley

[1] 1 Corinthians 6:11; [2] Ephesians 2:5; [3] 1 Corinthians 1:18; [4] Romans 5:9; [5] Romans 13:11b

21: A letter about the Lord's return

Dear Paul,

THERE is one aspect of your teaching which some Christians have been almost obsessive about but which most have neglected entirely. I'm thinking about your expectations concerning the second coming of Christ. How I wish I could talk with you and get a clearer idea not just of what you thought when you were on earth but what you think now.

As a theological student you would have been familiar with Jewish expectations of the Day of the Lord, when God would break in on human history. In addition to passages in the Jewish Scriptures there was plenty of other literature on the subject. Did you soak yourself in it and have a few late sessions of discussion with other students? I guess so.

Later, when you heard what Jesus said about his return I'm sure your expectations came into sharper focus.

When you wrote one of your earlier letters, to Christians at Thessalonica, there was the expectation that the second coming was imminent. I would like to have quizzed you about any possible development in your thought about this. I guess I would need to get my head around the fact (which you would know better than I) that with the Lord 'a day is like a thousand years and a thousand years as a day'. That wouldn't be easy for a time-bound mortal like me.

While there would be some signs, as the Lord himself said, the precise time of his return could not be known. It would be unexpected, like the coming of a thief in the night. The important thing was to be ready and blameless at his coming.

You obviously loved the thought of the Lord's return and it gave added incentive to you in your labours. If that coming was delayed it was an extension of the day of grace and provided further opportunity to win people for Jesus. At least, that's how I look at it and I think you did the same.

Clearly, you didn't see human existence as a *cul de sac.* History was going somewhere. Its consummation would be in Christ. History was *his story!* The whole creation was waiting for the great, divine event. For those in Christ, life was not a meaningless charade or a vicious circle but preparation for something greater. To take your own words to the Colossians: 'When Christ who is your life appears then you also will appear with him in glory.'[1]

Interestingly, you rounded off a letter to the Greek-speaking Christians in Corinth with the Aramaic phrase, *Maranatha* meaning, 'Come O Lord'.[2] It may have been a kind of watchword or password in your day. It spoke of a hope which many of us who 'love his appearing' still cherish. We believe with you that the trumpet will sound and Jesus will reign.

Yours sincerely,

Wesley

[1]Colossians 3:4; [2]1 Corinthians 16:22

43

22: A letter about judgment here and now

Dear Paul,

I SHOULD tell you that these days 'theological correctness' doesn't give much place to the idea of judgment. In fact, 'user-friendly' preachers tend to give the subject a wide berth. Yet the so-called 'gentle Jesus' had plenty to say about it and you didn't avoid it either. You even discoursed on righteousness, self-control and the judgment to come when you appeared in front of Governor Felix – not something most prisoners would think of doing when hauled before a 'high court judge'![1]

But while, without a doubt, you believed we will all be accountable to God in the life which is to come, I think you would agree that in some ways judgment may be upon us in this life. I've worked with people who lived lives of drunkenness and in a sense their sentence was written on their faces and judgment had been passed on the bodies they so long abused. God might have forgiven them but their bodies hadn't!

Judgment may also come in a moment of truth when people realise they have 'blown it' and wasted the hours and the powers given to them. Your name-sake Saul was one such, don't your think? He had so much going for him; he even became king of his country. Yet he was morally flawed and eventually came to a moment of truth when he passed judgment on himself and said, 'I have acted like a fool and erred greatly.'[2]

Would you agree something similar could have happened to another Saul – Saul of Tarsus? There you could have gone. But for

44

the grace of God you could easily have become bitter and twisted, despite all the natural gifts which were yours as a young man. As it was, you met Jesus on the highway and he saved you from yourself. Instead of being consumed by hatred you were filled with love; God's love flooded your soul.

Of course, it was a rocky road you trod. There were ups and downs and many hardships but when you were near the end, and able to look back, your mindset was very different from that of the other Saul. You said: 'I have fought the good fight, I have finished the race, I have kept the faith.'[3]

As I imagine you saying those words I get a tingling in my spine! Then I imagine you turning from the past and, in faith, lifting your eyes to the eternal future as you said: 'Now there is in store for me the crown of righteousness, which the Lord, the righteous Judge, will award to me on that day – and not only to me, but also to all who have longed for his appearing.'[4]

Do you remember saying that? I'm sure you do. And now you know that what you envisaged was no mirage. What you contemplated was not 'fool's gold', it was real.

One of the things I find about writing to someone who is out of this world is that it helps me lift my own vision and strengthen my sometimes faltering faith. I'm glad about that.

Yours sincerely,

Wesley

[1]Acts 24:25; [2]1 Samuel 26:21b; [3]2 Timothy 4:7; [4]2 Timothy 4:8

23: A letter about Heavenly bodies

Dear Paul,

IN some ways death seems to be the great unmentionable in polite conversation nowadays, as sex was to a previous generation. The one thing certain in life is death but many are not prepared to face it. It's said we all think everyone else is mortal but us! But it's clear that, for you, death was not a matter for morbidity or fear. Because of your faith you could meet it with a calm spirit and even keen anticipation.

In picturesque language you wrote to Timothy about the crown of righteousness which awaited you and other believers. As you said on another occasion when you wrote about the life to come, you could see only in part, like a reflection in one of the metal mirrors of your day. But now you have passed beyond time and space and you have a great advantage over those of us who are still earthbound.

Please be patient if what I write seems foolish in the light of your superior knowledge. Your written words are a lamp to our feet but they scarcely answer all the questions we might wish to ask. But there's no harm in asking, is there?

I've been reading what you wrote to the Corinthians about the resurrection of the body. Do I understand you to infer that in the after-life we will not merely be vague spirits but complete persons; not less than we are now but much more?

Our earthly bodies are means of expression and recognition. They are also adapted to our current earthly environment. But you wrote that while our spiritual bodies will have a certain continuity with our earthly bodies – as the flower has continuity with the seed which is sown in the earth – they will be adapted to our new environment and, as I understand it, perfectly express the redeemed 'selfhood' which will be ours. I think we will still be our recognisable selves but in a very different setting.[1]

Am I right in saying that our life after death will be essentially the same as our Christian life on earth, only carried on in new circumstances? Instead of bodies which might have become aged or diseased we will have bodies which are gloriously new. That will be a great relief for some. As you put it, that which is sown may be perishable but what will be raised will be imperishable. Right?

Of course, for us it is all a mystery, but, through faith, a mystery of light, not darkness. We don't mourn as those without hope. For the Christian the best is always yet to be. That's what you meant, isn't it?

You quoted treasured words from Scripture: 'No eye has seen, no ear has heard, no mind has conceived what God has prepared for those who love him.'[2]

Those words seem to speak of a loving God who has some marvellous surprises in store for us. As we remain in his waiting room we need not fear the coming consultation. God has good news for us. Because of Jesus we will be surprised by joy. Someone has said that at times we ought to wrestle with big themes, even if they throw us. I've probably been thrown, but I'll keep trying and praying and believing.

Yours sincerely,

Wesley

[1] *1 Corinthians 15:42-44;* [2] *1 Corinthians 2:9 (quoting Isaiah 64:4)*

24: A letter about different gifts

Dear Paul,

I BELIEVE you were divinely inspired, but for all that I'm sure some of your decisions as a leader were far from easy, or 'cut and dried' as we say. I discover that the word you used for the gift of administration actually means 'steersmanship'[1] and doubtless piloting the gospel ship was as tricky in your day as it is now. One mistake and a wreck would result.

You wrote a lot about spiritual gifts and drew up different lists of them. You don't appear to have thought any of the lists was exhaustive or exclusive. God's gifts are as many and varied as any situation may require and sovereign grace is ready to bestow. Is that right? Did you think that different churches should have different 'gift mixes' so that what's appropriate for one place might not be so in another? I would love to talk with you to make sure that I'm reading you rightly on this subject, particularly those aspects which have sometimes caused division in the Church and squabbling among God's children as to who should have which gifts.

You maintained that gifts are not merely for private gratification but for the building up of the Body of Christ which is the Church.[2] With some reservations, you seem to have allowed for public speaking in unintelligible tongues (with interpretation) at Corinth but you didn't promote this when writing to other churches under your direction. On the other hand prophecy, the telling forth of God's word, seems to have been a priority for you.

You told the Christians at Corinth that while you would have liked them all to speak in tongues you wished even more that they would prophesy. You claimed you had spoken in tongues more than anyone, but I wonder if this was as part of your private prayer, for you also said that in public you would 'rather speak five intelligible words to instruct others than ten thousand words in a tongue'.[3] You feared that if, in a service, everyone started speaking in tongues willy-nilly any unbeliever who wandered in might think the Christians were out of their minds.[4] Fair enough! Making the message clear and plain was obviously your main concern, as it is mine.

Some have claimed that if people don't speak in tongues they're not filled with the Spirit, but I have difficulty with that – as I think you would. After all, there's no hint of Jesus speaking in tongues, and if *anyone* was perfectly filled with the Spirit it was our Lord. We can't be more Christian than Christ! You taught that with regard to *gifts* there is something for everyone but, perhaps, not necessarily everything for anyone. However, when it comes to what you called the *fruit* of the Spirit (love, joy, peace and so on) I believe you would say they are all for all.[5] We can *all* be 'wholly sanctified'.[6]

Your teaching about holiness has been taken very seriously in the part of the Church to which I belong and my friends and I would acknowledge our indebtedness to you. Thank you!

Being a 'caretaker' – taking care of the Church – wasn't easy in your day and it's not easy now, with all the changes and cross-currents affecting the work. But it's good to have you as a mentor – one who has, in so many ways, been there and done that!

Gratefully yours,

Wesley

[1] *1 Corinthians 12:28b;* [2] *1 Corinthians 12:7, 18-20, 27-30;*
[3] *1 Corinthians 14:18, 19;* [4] *1 Corinthians 14:23;* [5] *Galatians 5:22;*
[6] *1 Thessalonians 5:23*

25: A letter about 'myself or the Lord?'

Dear Paul,

I NOTICE that addressing the Corinthians about marriage you differentiated between your own personal opinion and what you felt was a word from the Lord. You wrote, 'To the married I give this command (not I but the Lord) ... ' and 'To the rest I say this (I, not the Lord) ...'.[1] That might raise the question as to *how* divine inspiration came to you so that you could confidently proclaim something as being from God.

Perhaps it happened as you pored over the ancient Jewish Scriptures and saw how they were fulfilled in Christ. Did it also happen as you shared fellowship with other believers? Was there sudden illumination as you foot-slogged between one preaching appointment and another? I believe it was the Holy Spirit who gave you an *Amen* in your heart and assured you that what you were writing or speaking was the authentic word of God. And those who compiled what we now call the New Testament, along with millions of believers through the centuries, shared the same assurance. The same Spirit who inspired you in your writing inspires us in our reading of your letters today and leads us to give thanks for your continuing ministry.

As I read some of the great doctrines you proclaimed it's clear they were not merely human inventions 'plucked out of the air'; often they arose out of your own personal experience as a man in Christ. You could write to Rome: 'The Spirit himself testifies with our spirit that we are God's children.'[2] That was your testimony. You had wonderful head knowledge but you had heart knowledge as well. You not only knew *about* Christ but *knew him* and the power of his resurrection in a very personal way.[3]

You must have pondered long on the living, dying and rising of the Lord Jesus. You talked with those who had walked with him. You heard his gracious words repeated so often that you began to think like him.[4] Small wonder that your written words were in conformity with Christ the Living Word. They were authenticated in the light of the life of our Lord. You were his self-confessed slave and his mouthpiece.

Would you agree that in many ways you were a man of your time? Your patterns of speech were those of your particular era. Yet you were given words that ring true in every time. You were part of the current culture, yet the truth entrusted to you transcended the thought forms of your day.

We're told that Jesus taught with authority, and something of his authority was delegated to you as his ambassador. What you wrote was inspired – in-breathed – by the Holy Spirit, which is why we can hang on your words today. Am I right in thinking you would only wish to give God the glory for this?

Yours sincerely,

Wesley

[1] *1 Corinthians 7:10, 12;* [2] *Romans 8:16;* [3] *Philippians 3:10;* [4] *Philippians 3:9*

26: A letter about liberation from the bondage of decay

Dear Paul,

I'M sure you were a lover of nature. It's inconceivable that with your poetic mind you could have been oblivious to the beauty of flower and field and sunset as you trudged those many miles on missionary journeys. But such appreciation is not reflected in your writing to the extent it is in the teaching of our Lord. Doubtless, you would have said Amen to the words of the psalmist when he said the heavens declared the glory of God.[1] But were you also aware of what might be called nature's less acceptable face?

Nature can be cruel, 'red in tooth and claw', and it seems necessary for some species to prey upon others in order to survive. Did you wonder whether this was really part of God's ideal will? The thought has often exercised my mind and given me cause for reflection.

Then much of the beauty of nature is transient. Magnificent flowers may bloom only for a day. The glory of the sunset quickly passes, captured only in the memories of those who witness it. Change and decay is all around us in this world and you seem to have been very much aware of it.

Yet with poetic and prophetic vision you also seemed to envisage nature expectantly standing on tiptoe, waiting for 'the one far-off divine event to which the whole creation moves'. Despite the undoubted beauty which nature displays you were convinced there was something better in store.

Can I remind you of something you said in one of my favourite passages in your letter to the Christians in Rome? 'The creation waits in eager expectation for the sons of God to be revealed. For the creation was subjected to frustration, not by its own choice, but by the will of the one who subjected it, in hope that the creation itself will be liberated from its bondage to decay and brought into the glorious freedom of the children of God.'[2]

At that point I think you possibly left some of your readers behind. Your apostolic optimism knew no bounds. You were divinely inspired to write even greater things than you may have realised at the time. I wonder if, at the back of your mind, there was God's word in the book of Isaiah: 'Behold I will create new heavens and a new earth. The former things will not be remembered, nor will they come to mind.'[3]

At this point, as on many other occasions, I wish you could reply to my letter with some word to clear my clod-like brain. One day you may be in a position to put me right and make things clear. In the meantime I must rely on the Holy Spirit to provide enough light for the next step along the road that leads to the land of everlasting clearness, the ultimate state of blessedness prepared for the children of God. But I don't find this business of walking by faith easy. You understand, don't you?

Yours sincerely,

Wesley

[1]Psalm 19:1; [2]Romans 8:19-21; [3]Isaiah 65:17

27: A letter about those who have died

Dear Paul,

I'VE been having second thoughts and wondering if I should have written my letters to you in the style of the first rather than the 21st century. That would have meant putting the name of the sender at the beginning rather than the end of each letter (not a bad idea) and including various salutations as you did in your epistles.

On reflection, though, it's probably just as well for me to write in contemporary style, for while in one way you are a man from the past in another sense you span the centuries and are very much a 'today person' whose writings speak to our times. But I find it hard to get my head round the implications of my life being in a time frame while yours is not.

The question arises, how much are you are actually aware of what is happening in the world today? Can those who have died and gone to Heaven track the progress of people left behind?

Writing to Christians at Corinth you spoke of those who had 'fallen asleep' in Christ and would at the resurrection receive new bodies for old and find death swallowed up in victory.[1] However, the writer of the letter to the Hebrews – not you, some would say – may provide a picture of saints who have died being very much awake and aware of what is happening on earth. After a roll call of heroes of faith we read: 'Therefore, since we are surrounded by such a great cloud of witnesses, let us throw off everything that hinders and the sin that so easily entangles.'[2]

Those words conjure up for me a picture of the great 'spiritual olympians' of the past crowding the grandstands and cheering on the young hopefuls of the present. Is it really like that? If so, I'm sure you must be a cheerleader, not remote or removed but actively concerned about the progress of those still running the race with eyes fixed on Jesus.

But there are things which happen on earth which cause distress and it's said that Heaven is a place where there is no sorrow.[3] So how could the glorified saints know of such things without being saddened? Perhaps you would be in a position to reply that, with knowledge of events on earth there is given to those in Glory an ability to see the wider picture and a faculty to view things in the light of eternity. Is that it?

Your probing mind sought to explore the mysteries of life and death when you were on earth and you were given inspired insights to pass on. But there's still much to be revealed. What I believe to be certain, however, is that at death the redeemed are in the hands of God and have nothing to fear. We need not mourn as those without hope. A bereaved retiree confided to me: 'When I repeat my prayers at night I say, "Dear Lord, please give my love to Win" [his late wife]. Is that wrong?' I assured him that far from being wrong it was beautiful that he felt able to take everything (and everyone) to God in prayer.

What else could I say? Being human we may sometimes be muddled in our ideas but we have a Heavenly Father who understands and one day he will make everything plain. I'm sure you would agree with that.

Yours sincerely,

Wesley

[1] *1 Corinthians 15:18-21;* [2] *Hebrews 12:1;* [3] *Revelation 21:4*

28: A letter about the need for preaching

Dear Paul,

YEARS ago, preaching was described as 'thirty minutes to raise the dead' but nowadays some of us are expected to do the job in half the time! Even if we don't know how to finish we are required to know how to stop! I suspect you didn't feel the same time constraints. There was a famous occasion when you preached a long sermon and someone not only fell asleep but fell out of the window as well.[1] You might laugh now but it wouldn't have been funny at the time.

Preaching styles change and yours would have been influenced by the examples of the rabbis who taught you in your youth although, doubtless, you adapted your approach to circumstances as you found them, particularly among the Gentiles. All my life I've heard people say the day of preaching is over. I've never believed it and I'm sure you wouldn't either. You said God was pleased through the 'foolishness' of what was preached to save those who believed. Wonderful! God can turn the water of our words into the wine of his Word not merely because of our clever talking but by his Spirit. Thank you for saying so many things which have helped me with regard to preaching.

For example, you wrote to the Christians at Corinth: 'This all-surpassing power is from God and not from us.'[2] That has been brought home to me in that my preaching has sometimes appeared to be most effective when I've felt most inadequate. I may have felt like crawling off the platform, but, for all that, people have been saved and Jesus has been glorified, which is all that matters. Reading between the lines, I think it was sometimes like that with you.

You said, in the same passage; 'We do not preach ourselves but Jesus Christ as Lord.'[3] I take that to mean we shouldn't merely preach what we practise although we should seek to practise what we preach. The important thing is not to project ourselves but to lift up Christ. Right?

It could be that some Christians at Corinth didn't find your speaking impressive, but that was their problem. I'm sure they were wrong and that you were big enough to shrug off any negative comments, assured that God had been pleased to bless your labours. After all, if *he* smiles it might not matter who else frowns!

You urged Timothy to preach the Word.[4] For you, the written Word of God would have been what we now know as the Old Testament plus the oral traditions about Jesus still fresh in the memories of many of the people you met. We also see the God-breathed writings of what we call the New Testament (including your powerful letters) as God's Word and through them we learn about Christ, the Living Word. As some of us try to preach the Word in a world very different from the one you knew we are helped by your timeless advice. Once again, I can't thank you enough.

Yours sincerely,

Wesley

[1] *Acts 20:9;* [2] *2 Corinthians 4:7b;* [3] *2 Corinthians 4:5;* [4] *2 Timothy 4:2*

29: A letter about crossing into Europe

Dear Paul,

I KNEW a Christian leader who used to say there were days when all the angels seemed to be flying in the wrong direction. I know what he meant. To put it in another way, there are times when all doors seem to be closed and we feel very frustrated. Your friend Luke described a period when you might have felt that way and when you had to learn (as I certainly have) that at times the Holy Spirit closes some doors as well as opening others.

Dear Luke says that when you thought of conducting an evangelical campaign in the province of Asia the Holy Spirit stopped you, although the prospects appeared good. Likewise, when you would have entered Bithynia with the same purpose in mind, the Spirit of Jesus wouldn't allow it.[1] How did you feel about that? It must have seemed as though you were walking down a dark corridor with doors on the left and right bearing 'Do not enter' signs. What rational explanation could there be?

How did you get the message that you shouldn't go into those areas at that time? Were you unwell and, if so, did the Holy Spirit use that fact to head you in another direction? Did one of your companions have some clear guidance from the Lord or did you yourself feel the Spirit nudging you to keep going toward the coast? However it happened, eventually you came to what might have seemed a blank wall but where – surprise, surprise – there was a door of opportunity.

You will recall that when you reached the end of the road at Troas, in the middle of the night you had a dream which, fortunately, you were able to remember in the morning. You dreamt of a man from Macedonia urging you to cross the sea and take the gospel into Europe.[2] Who was the man in your vision? Some have suggested it was Luke, who seems to have just joined your party and may have been chatting to you over supper.

It's also been thought that it might have been someone from the past, the historical figure of the Macedonian Alexander the Great who had certainly left his mark, particularly on that part of the world (the full name of the place where you were was *Alexandrian Troas*). Who can tell? Dreams and visions can be strange at times. The important point is that through the vision you got the message, obediently caught a ship and took the gospel into Europe with incalculable consequences for the subsequent history of the world. Clearly, God the great strategist was at work and your line of communication with him was completely open. Wonderful!

I find pondering on your experience helpful. I've sometimes wondered what God was doing and questioned why things haven't turned out as *I* would have thought best. But like you, I guess, I've come to see that *he* knows best. In your letter to the Christians in Rome you put it beautifully: 'And we know that in all things God works for the good of those who love him, who have been called according to his purpose.'[3] I say Amen to that!

Yours sincerely,

Wesley

[1]*Acts 16:7;* [2]*Acts 16:9;* [3]*Romans 8:28*

30: A letter about being all things to all people

Dear Paul,

I THINK it's generally true that if we care we will communicate. I know if I had fallen in love with a girl who didn't understand my language I would have found some way of communicating how I felt! If that meant language classes then that wouldn't have stopped me. Certainly, your passion about mission made *you* go to great lengths in order to win people for Christ. You wrote to people in the city of Corinth, 'I have become all things to all men so that by all possible means I might save some.'[1] You were ready to do whatever it took.

While maintaining continuity of principle, you were prepared for almost unlimited adaptation of method. For Jesus' sake you were ready to move out of your comfort zone and identify with people of vastly different cultures from your own. That must have taken a Spirit-inspired flexibility which might not have come easily for someone of your temperament and religious background.

Frankly, it's not always easy for some of us these days. At times we face a cultural chasm which is hard to get over. The language of the holy place may come more easily to us than that of the market place when we speak about our faith – and that may lead to a communication problem. Establishing relationships with unbelievers can be difficult but your example provides a challenge and incentive.

To 'save some' you were prepared to stretch many of your preferences and prejudices to breaking point. You declared that you were willing to identify with all kinds and conditions of people for the sake of their salvation, and in this, of course, you were following the example of our Lord, who was seen as the friend of publicans and sinners.

In order to win people you were prepared to be like them in many ways but, paradoxically, in some important respects, in order to help them you had to be unlike them. You had to dare to be different and have a spiritual quality which they did not have. It was because you were a 'man in Christ' that you had something to offer those who were dying spiritually. Identification without Christian identity would have been fruitless, but you managed to maintain the critical balance.

Looking back through the mists of many years I can follow your tracks quite easily and try to follow you as you sought to follow our Lord. Our times may be different, circumstances may have changed, but it strikes me that what's required for the advance of the gospel may not be all that different.

You knew all about 'friendship evangelism' and the importance of getting alongside people to win them. What we may sometimes think of as new theories about church growth may not really be new at all. You were aware of some of them in your day but we need to rediscover them for ourselves. It's good to be able to use your experience as a sounding board and share some of your Spirit-inspired insights. Thank you!

Yours sincerely,

Wesley

1 Corinthians 9:22

31: A letter about the Church as people

Dear Paul,

IT was long after your time that Christians began to erect buildings especially designed for worship. Now, you would be surprised to know that when many people think of a church they have bricks and mortar in mind. They think of buildings, often of a distinctive shape, where special services are held. But, just as there is more to a home than a house, the Church is more than a location where gatherings take place. You made it very clear that the Church is people.

I believe that in your day Christians met for worship in caves, beside rivers and in each others' homes. You wrote about the 'Church in the house' – the 'Church domestic' we might call it – in the house of Philemon[1] for example and, wherever they moved, in the home of Aquila and Priscilla[2].

Although we now have our church buildings there is in these days a rediscovery of the value of small groups meeting in homes. Some unbelievers are rather nervous about entering a church building but are more ready to accept the invitation of a friendly neighbour and share refreshments followed by Bible study and prayerful discussion in a home.

For years my wife and I held such meetings in our house each week and the fellowship proved very helpful. You should know that we have gone through most of your letters, sentence by sentence, and thanked God again and again for your continuing ministry. If it is not too presumptuous to say so, we almost felt you were one of us.

For much of your life you had no place to call your own where you could invite people to share in this way but you would certainly have joined such groups in the various places you visited. I can visualise you singing and praying, pondering the Scriptures and explaining how Christ fulfilled many of the ancient prophecies. I wonder if sometimes people brought out one of your letters and asked you to explain the points you made. I think you would have welcomed such opportunities, for, however good the writing may be, there's nothing like person-to-person contact. You would have been a great pastor and you certainly worked hard not only to establish congregations but to build up individual believers in the faith.

In some countries governments have banned the Christian religion and closed down church buildings. But one dictator who did just that had to exclaim with rage that the peasants had built new churches in their hearts! When persecution has raged, the faith has often been maintained by clandestine meetings in the homes of Christians who risk their lives to keep the faith.

You would be familiar with this and will be heartened to know the work and witness continues and that, despite all setbacks, the Church worldwide is numerically stronger than it has ever been. Hallelujah!

Yours hopefully,

Wesley

¹Philemon 1:1, 2; ²1 Corinthians 16:19

32: A letter about God's commission

Dear Paul

YOU may realise your letters have been translated into many languages. In my native tongue there have also been new translations and paraphrases. That's just as well because language is always developing and it's important for people to receive the truth of the gospel in terms they find easy to understand. Reading one of the modern versions I saw that you wrote to Timothy: 'Keep your commission free from stain.'[1]

That really got to me and reminded me of a treasured document in my possession – the Salvation Army officer's commission given to me when I began my ministry more than 50 years ago. Time has left its mark on that piece of paper as well as on the one whose name is inscribed upon it! It has yellowed over the years but, by the grace of God, what it represents has not been stained.

You wrote to the Christians in Corinth: 'We put no stumbling block in anyone's path, so that our ministry will not be discredited.'[2] Am I right in thinking you felt that what people read in your life makes more impression than what they read in your letters? You were anxious that there be no credibility gap in your character, nothing that would make acceptance of your ministry more difficult.

For years I have hung on your every word and gather that you never lost a sense of wonder about your commission as an ambassador of Jesus Christ.[3] You were sometimes 'an ambassador in chains' but obviously you could not have imagined a higher calling or a more significant mandate than that you received from Jesus Christ. A similar conviction has steadied me through the years. My commission has invested life with meaning it would otherwise have lacked, and for that I'm deeply grateful. I'm a very ordinary person but if for one soul I have been a 'God-send' then that is awesome, to use a colloquialism favoured by modern youth.

Nowadays the air is literally filled with messages we can tune in and listen to – good, bad and indifferent. But people need to hear words which have the authority of authenticity. Just as in your day, they need a word from the Lord. Like you, I believe every Christian is called to declare that word in one way or another.

You said you were determined to know nothing among people except Christ crucified. He was at the forefront of your message and all you said was backed by the example of your own lifestyle. That was what made your ministry so powerful. Without a divine commission we could all be like babbling salespeople in the marketplace of words. But realising we are sent by God makes all the difference.

Yours sincerely,

Wesley

¹1 Timothy 6:14; ²2 Corinthians 6:3; ³Ephesians 6:20

33: A letter about making doctrine attractive

Dear Paul,

IT'S wonderful that you were able to open your mind to divine revelation, draw on your own spiritual experience and then lay down some of the foundations of Christian doctrine accepted by millions today. Did you realise you were writing about truths that would transcend human wisdom and inspire countless hearts? The very idea is awesome.

Having explored the heights and depths of spirituality you often turned to the practical details of living out the Christian life, and I really like that. It's said some people are so Heavenly minded they are of no earthly use, but no one could say that about you. Even when you were reaching toward the skies you kept your feet on the ground.

For example, I've been going through your letter to Titus. Reading between the lines it seems that young pastor wanted a change of appointment, because the people in Crete were not the easiest to handle. However, it appears the reasons he might have given for moving were also your reasons for asking him to stay on, so he might give the people sound instruction and they in turn might adorn the doctrine, or, as you put it, 'make the teaching about God our Saviour attractive'.[1]

No disrespect, but I would have expected you to say the doctrines would adorn the people or make them more attractive but you put it the other way around. That made me think and my mind went running along the following lines: doctrines may be like the plans for a house or the score for a piece of music. A few people may enjoy poring over plans or studying a score but most want to see the actual house or hear the living music. In the same way I think you wanted people to see doctrines translated into lifestyle. Right?

Still puzzling over your words I came at them from another angle. I've read that if pearls are hidden away in dry conditions they lose their lustre, but when they are worn, the natural oils in the wearer's skin nourish them and enhance their beauty. Like pearls, Christian doctrines are meant to be worn or lived out and become more attractive as a result.

I'm sorry to say that for some people the doctrine of holiness, for example, seems rather dull, despite all the wonderful things you and others have written about it. But when people really see it shining through a fine character that's different. The doctrine comes alive and people are reminded of the beauty of Jesus himself. I hope I'm not taking liberties with the things you wrote. Spiritually and intellectually you leave me far behind but at least I want to catch the gist of what you were saying long ago and see how it makes sense for those of us trying to follow the Lord now.

Lots of unbelievers never open the Scriptures and are unfamiliar with your wonderful letters but for good or ill they read our lives and form an opinion about Christianity from what they see in us. We want to make the faith more, not less, attractive to them. I can almost hear you say Amen to that.

Yours sincerely,

Wesley

¹Titus 2:10

34: A letter about whether we've accomplished anything at all

Dear Paul,

AT times it seems your letters have my name on them! They address issues which have a personal application to matters I encounter in my ministry to others. For example, I spoke to a man who had composed a lot of fine music for use in Christian worship but who said, 'I sometimes wonder whether I have ever accomplished anything at all.' Obviously he was having a bad day and in that he would not have been alone!

To some Christians in Corinth who may have been feeling down you wrote: 'Always give yourself fully to the work of the Lord, because you know that your labour in the Lord is not in vain.'[1]

As so often happens, your thoughts triggered thoughts of my own. Do you agree that even we servants of God can get discouraged because we often don't know how much our service has meant to other people? We preach our sermons or give practical service but have no clue as to how people are affected. The devil would suggest it's all been a dead loss, but he is the 'father of lies'.[2] I received a letter from someone I had heard nothing of in nearly 40 years. When I knew him he was a delinquent youth in trouble with the authorities and all my efforts to help him seemed to have failed. Then, after all those years, he wrote from another country to say he was active in the Lord's work and wanted to thank me for what I had done for him. That was humbling, but a great encouragement. Praise the Lord!

I don't know whether this was your experience, but we sometimes feel our labour is in vain because we don't realise how much it has meant to *us*. In the unlikely event of no one else being blessed, at least our own hearts have been strengthened and our wayward natures disciplined as we have sought to serve. When we have visited the sick we may have been stirred by their faith and fortitude. The messages we prepare for others may bring challenge to our own spirit. I'm sure joy in your heart must often have been kindled as you wrote your letters designed to inspire others. That would have made those letters worthwhile even if they had never been sent on their way by messenger.

Sometimes, too, we mistakenly think our labour is in vain because we don't realise how much it means to *God*. I find it humbling that the great Creator and Governor of the universe accepts and values the service of mere mortals. If what we offer brings joy to the heart of God how could it be in vain? Others may overlook our efforts or misconstrue our motives but God knows and appreciates every sincere effort to serve him. That's what really matters.

You will remember that in the passage from which I have taken some of your words you were thinking of the life to come as well as this life. I believe you meant we should not only see our service as being 'in the Lord' but should view it in the light of eternity. Thank you for giving us that perspective.

Yours sincerely,

Wesley

[1] 1 Corinthians 15:58; [2] John 8:44

35: A letter about military discipline

Dear Paul

YOU would need no convincing that war is a bad business. It was horrible in your time but now we have weapons of mass destruction which make things even worse. It's diabolical but whole cities can be wiped out in an instant. In your day the power of Rome kept a lid on many possible local conflicts. The Roman Peace was enforced, frontiers were open and you and others could take the gospel along the great new roads in a way previously impossible.

You were a man of peace but you were able to get along with men of war, like Julius the centurion in the Imperial Regiment, who accompanied you on your journey to Rome.[1] I think you admired the discipline of soldiers and felt something of that kind was needed by those who served Christ. What I would describe as the journalist in you enlisted the image of the soldier and pressed it into the service of Jesus, and many of us have taken your cue and done something similar. You said to Timothy: 'Endure hardship with us like a good soldier of Christ Jesus.'[2] You knew, better than most, that for the Christian the going could get tough and it was important to be 'strong in the grace that is in Christ Jesus'[3] and not be a spiritual wimp.

The Lord didn't promise that everything would be easy. He said that in the world we would have tribulation, and you had more than your fair share of that. By comparison with your experience, I've had it easy and should be ashamed if I have faltered at all. You emphasised that a soldier should beware of entanglements or getting 'involved in civilian affairs' and only be concerned to 'please his commanding officer'.[4]

That was using military terminology to lay it on the line for someone starting out as a Christian leader and I've often been glad to borrow your words to challenge myself as well as others.

You had no doubt that there was a real war on and could certainly identify the enemy, whereas some Christians today are a bit fuzzy about who or what they are fighting, almost as if they are just playing at soldiers. You said in your letter to the Ephesians: 'For our struggle is not against flesh and blood but … against the spiritual forces of evil.'[5] I understand that when you wrote that you were in prison, probably chained by the wrist to a Roman guard. It would be very natural if, as you looked at the soldier at your side, you were inspired by the sight of his apparel and accoutrements to write to your fellow Christians, 'Put on the full armour of God' – likening the various parts of the guard's equipment to the spiritual resources needed by soldiers of Jesus.

Your use of the military metaphor reminds us that we are all called to active service. There are foes to face but there is grace sufficient. As I think of you writing under house arrest, or perhaps by this time from a dank and dirty cell with the threat of execution hanging over your head, your words are like a trumpet call. Thank you!

Yours gratefully,

Wesley

[1]*Acts 27:1, 43;* [2]*2 Timothy 2:3;* [3]*2 Timothy 2:1;* [4]*2 Timothy 2:4;* [5]*Ephesians 6:12;* [6]*Ephesians 6:11*

36: A letter about social service

Dear Paul,

I'M nonplussed by those Christians who suggest the Church should engage only in 'spiritual ministry' and not get involved in social outreach. Surely they can't claim to be more 'spiritual' than Jesus who was not only into evangelism in the narrow sense of the term but social action as well, feeding the hungry and healing the sick. Clearly, his mission was not only to the soul of a person but to the whole of a person, indeed to the whole of society. It seems natural that our mission should be equally comprehensive.

In his short history of the Early Church, Dr Luke described the setting up of the first social department of the Church, following the Jewish tradition of care for the poor and needy and carrying on the holistic ministry of our Lord.[1] I notice that those in charge had to be full of the Spirit and wisdom, obviously in order to ensure that even the dispensing of material assistance would be spiritually motivated.

It doesn't appear that you were personally involved in this kind of work, though I don't for one moment think you would have felt above it or disinclined to help if the need arose. However, your main roles were in preaching and writing and administration of the Church at large. But you certainly endorsed and encouraged social ministry, didn't you? Writing to the church in Galatia you said you were eager to promote a collection for the poor in Jerusalem.[2] In your list of gifts of the Spirit in your letter to the Romans, practical service is given an honoured place[3], which is not surprising given the example of our Lord who took a bowl and towel and washed his disciples' feet[4]. Jesus blessed the 'sacrament of service' and said that anything done to help the needy was done for him.[5]

Through modern means of communication we can now see pictures of war and famine and sickness all over the world. It is rather overwhelming at times and we wonder what we can do. The temptation is to feel that because we can't do *everything* we can't do *anything*.

I'm sure that if you were around you would be doing a great job organising collections for refugees and starving children – in addition to your preaching and writing. You had a heart to care and for Jesus' sake you were ready to embrace both spiritual and physical need. To the Christians at Corinth, you spoke about both the ministry and the message of reconciliation.[6] I think that what you had in mind would have included both social salvation and spiritual regeneration.

No doubt you felt as I do that the greatest service we can do for anyone is to introduce them to Jesus, but for his sake we should also be concerned about the totality of human need and be just as anxious to serve in any and every way possible.

Yours sincerely,

Wesley

[1]Acts 6:3; [2]Galatians 2:10; [3]Romans 12:7, 8; [4]John 13:5; [5]Matthew 25:40; [6]2 Corinthians 5:18, 19

37: A letter about 'fear which has said its prayers'

Dear Paul,

YOU seem to have 'got it all together' to a remarkable degree. You were able to face wild animals and wild men, persecution and privation – a whole catalogue of catastrophes – without flinching.[1] But I wonder whether it was always like that. You come across as an 'iron man' but I'd be surprised if at times you weren't as scared as I would have been in your place. You were only human after all!

It's not that I doubt your bravery – that's beyond question – but courage is the conquest of fear, not the absence of it. Don't you think that, at times, we *should* be fearful – of going too near a fire or the edge of a cliff, for example? But we need to overcome our fear in pursuit of a greater good. I think you would agree, because you often demonstrated that.

You might feel that what took most courage was not the facing of a sudden threat or emergency but the enduring of prolonged pressure. It must have been difficult for you to 'keep your cool' when former friends in Judaism sniped at you, and even more difficult when fellow Christians belittled your efforts or misconstrued your motives. The wounds we receive 'in the house of our friends' are sometimes most hurtful. So how did you manage? I'd like to learn your secret in order to follow your example.

I have a feeling that your bravery was fed by your faith.[2] Your courage was 'fear which had said its prayers'. Having feared the worst you were able to see beyond it to the best, which is always yet to be.

I think of the time when you were on a sinking ship and even the professional sailors were in a state of panic. You stood on the heaving deck and declared: 'Keep up your courage, men, for I have faith in God.'³ Across the centuries and above the howling storms I fancy I still hear your words. They must have put new heart into those around you and they do the same for me.

Of course, you can now view in the light of eternity the things which frightened you on earth. You may have a different perspective entirely – as I hope to have one day. It's said that perfect love casts out fear. That must be just one of the blessings of Heaven. I'm sure there are many others.

I try to imagine what you're doing these days. I can't imagine you being inactive. In addition to offering praise and worship to our Lord are you giving service and enjoying fellowship 'around the throne of God'? I wonder what else Heaven holds for you. The sound of music, perhaps. And what about laughter? Are songs of praise punctuated by holy hilarity?

I don't know, but I recall that you quoted the words: 'No eye has seen, no ear has heard, no mind has conceived what God has prepared for those who love him.'⁴ You were a 'brave heart' who went forward with confidence from this life to the next and I intend to follow in your footsteps.

Yours sincerely,

Wesley

¹1 Corinthians 15:32; 2 Corinthians 1:8; ²Romans 8:35;
³Acts 27:25; ⁴1 Corinthians 2:9

75

38: A letter about working with the saints below

Dear Paul,

IT seems some of your friends at Corinth wanted to regard you as a cult figure, or at least the leader of a faction within the Church. However, you wanted none of that and declared that you and other leaders were simply slaves of Christ 'entrusted with the secret things of God'.[1]

You used a word which originally referred to slaves who laboured on the lower of the three banks of oars on a trireme, or warship, in your time. How those men must have strained every muscle to wield the cumbersome oars and propel their heavy vessel through turbulent seas! In a different way your own labours to keep the gospel ship on course were also strenuous in the extreme. Taken seriously, leadership within the Church can never be a soft option, as you obviously found – and as I have found too.

Like those slaves, you felt you were a man under authority. You were no longer concerned to 'do your own thing'. You had gladly accepted the lordship of Jesus Christ and were compelled by love. And you were quite ready to work as part of a team with colleagues like Peter and Apollos. I like that.

Oarsmen have to find a common rhythm and work together. Uncoordinated effort is likely to be dissipated and ineffective. I often say it is teamwork which makes the dream work, but I've known some brothers and sisters in the Church who find it very difficult to work with other people. I guess you had the same problem with a few people despite them having your example as well as your precepts to guide them.

Some might say:

To live in love with the saints above will surely be such glory,
But to work below with the saints I know is quite a different
* story!*

There are those who are naturally loners and individualists and it may not be easy for them to join forces with others. But as an old saying has it, 'What we're not by nature we can become by grace.' Do you agree? In many situations cooperation is not optional but essential for spiritual victory. Happily, the Spirit of God can make it possible

As I pore over your words I sense you were obviously committed to 'servant leadership' for you stressed repeatedly the importance of working together as well as working with God. It seems your particular role was often to start a church and then move on to another situation. But your labour would have been in vain if it had not been for others who came after you and consolidated the position. That was something you were glad to recognise when you wrote to the Corinthian church and referred to the work of Apollos who followed you and, with the blessing of God, developed your work.[2]

I like people who are big enough to pay tribute to their successors (or predecessors) in the ministry, and that's just one of many things I admire in you.

Yours sincerely,

Wesley

[1] 1 Corinthians 4:1; [2] 1 Corinthians 3:6

77

39: A letter about statistics

Dear Paul,

EVANGELISTS sometimes become preoccupied with numbers, judging their success or failure according to the number of people who register decisions for Christ in a public way. It's a natural thing to do and I've done it myself, but spiritually it can be wide of the mark, and in the light of eternity it will be seen as such. There were occasions when crowds flocked to listen to our Lord but the time also came when the statistics didn't look good at all.[1]

Can metaphysical matters be measured by mathematical means? Is it possible to quantify spiritual response in statistical terms? Some of the results of spiritual commitment may be measured but who can gauge the commitment itself? You, Paul, may now be in a position to judge these things from an eternal perspective, so I wish I could learn your mind on the matter.

There were times when many people responded to your gospel appeal. But were there times for you when the visible response was meagre? Would your experience at Athens be a case in point? You were taken to the *Areopagus,* an exclusive court which had supreme authority in religious matters and power to arrange public lectures and exercise some control in the interests of public order.

If it's not presumptuous to praise an apostle, I think you gave a splendid address in those circumstances but your friend Dr Luke records that the response appeared limited. Some people sneered and others simply said they would listen again at some other time. However, a few believed, 'among them was Dionysius, a member of the *Areopagus,* and a woman named Damaris'.[2] There have been various suggestions as to why Damaris was mentioned by name but nothing very definite. However, it seems Dionysius had the status of a high court judge, being a member of a select group of about 30 people. So on what might not have seemed one of your best days there was at least one notable convert or 'trophy of grace'.

I wonder if it was he who gave Luke an account of what you said on that occasion, if you hadn't handed over your own notes for incorporation into the historical record. Tradition has it that Dionysius later became a bishop and died a martyr's death. He may have been just one of a small number in Athens who took you seriously but through him your influence may have spread far and wide, like the ripples caused by a stone thrown into a pond. I'm one of many preachers who have sometimes felt disheartened when there seems to have been few, if any, converts after hard labour. We preach for a verdict and are then dismissed out of hand by many of our listeners. But who can tell what may have been accomplished?

I remember how someone recording the number of 'seekers' after a preaching service added, as a throw-away thought, '... and one lad'. But that lad later became a powerful leader of God's people and brought a considerable addition to the influence of the Church. Sometimes when we feel we have done least good, God may have done most! We can only do our best and leave the rest to him, can't we? I guess that's what you had to do.

Yours sincerely,

Wesley

¹John 6:60; ²Acts 17:34

40: A letter about the call to sacrificial ministry

Dear Paul,

WHEN I interviewed a number of fine people who felt called to a particular Christian ministry I listened to their accounts of how God had laid his hand upon them and was moved to remember the pivotal moment when I was myself conscious of such a calling. As a result of my saying 'yes' to God my life has been so fulfilling and I'm glad that others continue to take up the baton and run with it.

Am I right in thinking that you also loved to talk of the time when you became aware of what has been called 'the ordination of the nail-pierced hands'? It didn't happen in a sanctuary but on a dusty road. Your friend Luke said that after the risen Christ had made himself known to you he said, 'Now get up and go ...'[1] an echo of his command to the disciples to go into all the world.[2] For you it was a case of 'first stop Damascus' and await further instructions. For others the place names are different but the spiritual direction the same.

Do you recall giving your testimony before King Agrippa? You declared that the Lord said: 'I have appeared to you to appoint you as a servant and as a witness of what you have seen of me.'[3] That was an awesome appointment but you took it without equivocation. You had been a proud Pharisee but you became a servant or slave of all. You later told the Christians in Corinth that you accepted such a calling for Jesus' sake.[4]

The love of Christ compelled you to do what you did. That was what drove you, so when you reached what you thought was breaking point you didn't break. You were called not merely to propound a theory but to witness to something validated in your own experience. You had become a new creature in Christ. Old things had passed away. A new day had dawned. You would never be the same again – and the change that took place in your life can happen to any man or woman. That was news too good not to be true! And the thrill of it still throbs through your writings and helps inspire other hearts.

You'll be sorry to learn that for some years now there has been a dearth of candidates for the ministry. People tend to reject what may be an itinerant and sacrificial life in favour of a more affluent and settled existence. But in some countries the tide is turning. The lure of materialism seems to be wearing thin. People are finding that it's living for a cause that makes life worth living. The Cross is the attraction and the hardness provides the challenge.

I'm sure you could relate to this. You had everything needed to make a name for yourself in Judaism. The sky was the limit for someone with your intellect and drive. But Jesus stopped you in your tracks and then caused a 'U' turn in your life. You found your true destiny and subsequently helped millions of others to find theirs. I can't thank you enough.

Yours sincerely,

Wesley

¹Acts 9:6; ²Matthew 28:19; ³Acts 26:16; ⁴2 Corinthians 4:5

41: A letter about prayer and holiness

Dear Paul,

IT seems that while many people pay lip service to the importance of praying, some find it difficult to move beyond perfunctory prayers to vital prayer. I wonder whether that's why, in my experience at least, attendance at prayer meetings nowadays tends to be sparse. The fear of many is that such gatherings will merely consist of vain repetitions, and be ineffectual, if not boring. It's clear from your letters that prayer was very important to you. You provided the churches with excellent teaching on the subject and some examples of wonderfully exalted prayer. But were there times when you, too, found prayer difficult? I wouldn't be surprised.

Writing to the believers in Rome you confessed that 'we do not know what we ought to pray'.[1] Was that because you wondered what might or might not be appropriate to say to the Lord? Were there times when what you called 'the care of the churches' and the general pressures of life numbed your mind and made prayer difficult? Did even you sometimes find it hard to express how you felt?

If that was so or not, you were led to write that at such times the Spirit himself interposes to intercede for us. As a mother might pray for the unborn baby unable to pray for him or herself so, as you put it, 'the Spirit intercedes for the saints in accordance with God's will'[2]. That helps me a lot when my thoughts wander and at the throne of grace I find myself lost for words.

I've also been unpacking something you said to your people in Thessalonica. You told them to 'pray continually'.[3] But I'm sure you didn't mean those people should spend their lives on their knees.

In the same letter you said people should work with their hands. In other words, laziness should not be cloaked in piety. Am I right in thinking that while you believed in setting aside time for specific prayer you also felt the whole of life can be an offering and a sacrifice of praise?

I know little about your trade of tent making but I can imagine that while you were working at it your thoughts would have been constantly turning to God. You would have prayed with your hands as well as your lips. Perhaps the reason why prayer is sometimes difficult is that we don't generally maintain a high enough standard of thinking. It's all but impossible to snap out of low thinking and engage in high praying. After writing to people in Philippi about prayer you said they should think on things which were pure and true and lovely.[4] Were you perhaps inferring that the price of vital prayer is habitual self discipline in thought?

If so, it strikes me that effective prayer and holiness must go together; God listens to what we are as well as to what we say. As always, even a few of your words can set off a whole train of challenging thought in my mind – which is a good reason for believing you were truly inspired. I'm sure God is now blessing you in ways beyond my imagining.

Yours sincerely,

Wesley

[1]Romans 8:26b; [2]Romans 8:27; [3]1 Thessalonians 5:17; [4]Philippians 4:8

42: A letter about 'godly graffiti'

Dear Paul,

I'M one of many who like to display an ancient Christian symbol in use quite early in the history of the Church. It's the sign of a fish, which appeared as a form of 'godly graffiti' on the walls of caves where Christians hid in times of persecution. As you know, the word *ichthus* means fish and its letters provide initials for the words which translate as Jesus Christ, Son of God, Saviour. A passage in the book of Deuteronomy forbids making an image of a fish[1] – or any other creature – but early Christians saw no harm in using a secret sign which testified to their faith. Is that right?

When persecuted believers saw the scrawled sign of the fish they were encouraged to know they were not alone: others believed as they did, and knew the same Lord and Saviour. That was mightily encouraging. The simple sign lifted their spirits.

Did you ever feel like the prophet Elijah who at one time wondered whether he was the only true believer left? Certainly, as you moved around the pagan world of your day you would have welcomed anything which indicated that others shared a faith similar to yours. We can all be strengthened by a sense of solidarity with others of like heart and mind.

The part of the Church to which I belong has long encouraged its members to wear a uniform which indicates the wearer is a follower of Jesus. I spoke to a woman who said she belonged to another branch of the Church and was sometimes tempted to miss assembling for worship. But when she saw a friend of mine walking down the street in his uniform she was challenged to do what she knew she should. There was something sacramental about the uniform. It was a sign which gave silent testimony to a personal faith and that was good.

You told Timothy: 'Do not be ashamed to testify about our Lord'[2] and, like you, I believe Christians should be ready publicly to declare their allegiance to Jesus by every means available. After all, if Christ is not ashamed to own us with all our imperfections we should not be ashamed to own the Christ in whom even a secular judge could find no fault.

I heard of a man who wore a bent nail in the lapel of his smart business suit because this gave him opportunities to answer people's curious questions by speaking of his Lord and the way he was nailed to the Cross. Although it might not be everyone's choice of symbol, that simple sign served a useful purpose – like the sign of the fish scrawled on a wall or written on a letter.

You told Christians in Galatia that you bore on your body the marks of the Lord Jesus.[3] Did you have in mind signs of physical suffering endured for Christ which might also have brought opportunities to tell inquirers about the gospel you sought to proclaim? I'm sure you would have welcomed anything which gave opportunities to witness for the Lord.

Yours sincerely,

Wesley

[1]*Deuteronomy 4:18;* [2]*2 Timothy 1:8;* [3]*Galatians 6:17*

43: A letter about cheerful giving

Dear Paul,

A GROUP of singers complained to me because they felt the worshipful atmosphere brought into a meeting through their singing was spoilt when I followed their item with the collection. They were good people and I respected their point of view. But I don't think *you* would have had a problem with that order of meeting. Writing to the Christians at Corinth you reached high altitudes of inspiration on the subject of the resurrection then, suddenly, you brought your readers down to earth with a bump by writing: 'Now about the collection …'.[1] The spiritual and the practical, the worship and the giving went together as far as you were concerned. The financial contributions of Christians were to be regular and truly proportionate to income.

You wrote very carefully but I wouldn't be surprised if some people bridled. The part of the person where people keep their purse is often very sensitive! Obviously, a collection for the poor associated with the church in Jerusalem was close to your heart. Did you realise you used nine different words to describe it? I have wondered whether there were church politics involved in asking Gentile Christians to help the Church's headquarters in Jerusalem, where they were obviously strapped for cash.

Certainly, you made it clear that the implications were spiritual as well as financial. Giving was good for the soul. It was a way in which Christians could extend their influence to places they couldn't go to in person. It helped strengthen solidarity between the churches.

You knew Jews used the same word to describe both 'almsgiving' and 'righteousness' and you possibly thought that Christians saved by grace should not be behind their legalistic brethren in Judaism when it came to giving. Like you, I feel that if we have full hearts we should be ready to empty our pockets – lovingly not grudgingly. You said the Lord loves *cheerful* givers[2] and from the Greek word you used we get our word hilarious.

Hilarious givers may be rare! There is not usually a hallelujah heard when the collection is announced.

It was shrewd, writing to the possibly self-important church at Corinth, to cite the example of the poor churches in Macedonia and say: 'Out of the most severe trial, their overflowing joy and their extreme poverty welled up in rich generosity ... they urgently pleaded with us for the privilege of sharing.'[3]

But you made it clear that the supreme example of the grace of giving comes from Jesus. You wrote: 'You know the grace of our Lord Jesus Christ, that though he was rich, yet for your sakes he became poor, so that you through his poverty might become rich.'[4] Those inspired words still make a powerful appeal today and I'm glad to say I find in many places an increased awareness of the importance of giving sacrificially for the Lord's work. What's more, that seems a feature of all the growing churches. You wouldn't be surprised about that, I'm sure.

Yours sincerely,

Wesley

[1] 1 Corinthians 16:1; [2] 2 Corinthians 9:7; [3] 2 Corinthians 8:3, 4;
[4] 2 Corinthians 8:9

44: A letter about change versus tradition

Dear Paul,

SPIRITUALLY it's possible for our minds to become as cracked and dry as the discarded wineskins you saw from time to time. However, miraculously, our minds *can* be renewed. You wrote to the Christians in Rome: 'Do not conform any longer to the pattern of this world, but be transformed by the renewing of your mind.'[1] As was so often case, the doctrine you proclaimed was supported by the experience you enjoyed. It was amazing that a rigorous Pharisee could become supple enough in mind to accommodate the inclusion of Gentiles in the Church, with all the implications of that. You not only accepted change but became an agent of change and helped to ensure that what might have remained a sect of Judaism became a faith for the world.

Where there is life there is change, that's always been the case, but the rate of change has accelerated in recent days as a result of advances in technology, among other things. There is change in the Church as well as in the world. Young people particularly are opting for changes in the form of worship while other people prefer the traditional forms with which they are familiar. Ministers are having to provide a balance. It's good to report that there are more Christians in the world than ever before, with the Church on a huge victory march in some countries. But it seems the good seed doesn't do as well in affluent soil. Certainly, in some richer countries the Church is in decline, with people distracted from church attendance by materialism and sporting pursuits.

Not every change is for the best but it's important to find the best in every change and many congregations are doing that. While maintaining continuity of principle they are using adaptation of method. Some are able to use modern means of communication. You would be amazed that it's now possible to address simultaneously more people than you addressed throughout your ministry – although of course, you subsequently have reached millions through your writing, and that ministry continues to go from strength to strength.

As in your day, and following the example of the Lord, many congregations are engaging in practical community service – not as an alternative to the gospel but as an expression of it. Service and evangelism are going hand in hand. But the renewal of the Church can only come through the renewing of minds by the Spirit. God grant it will happen more and more!

Yours sincerely

Wesley

[1]*Romans 12:2*

45: A letter about telling the truth kindly

Dear Paul,

CHRISTIANS don't always see eye to eye, and that goes for apostles as well as the rest of us. Writing to the Galatian churches you said you had opposed Peter to his face on what you felt was a matter of principle.[1] There was no pussyfooting as far as you were concerned. What was wrong had to be challenged and you didn't hold back.

It's said that some people will slap your back to your face and slap your face to your back, but clearly you were frank and upfront in what you had to say. You told it the way you saw it. But I'm sure that although you and Peter disagreed you tried hard to avoid being disagreeable. You practised what you preached to your friends at Ephesus about 'speaking the truth in love'[2], thereby growing up in Christ rather than being petulant and childish in the way some people can be.

There are times when it's our Christian duty to rebuke or criticise but I've learnt from your letters that wrapping the criticism in a compliment makes it more acceptable. A sugar coating on a bitter pill makes it less hard to swallow but not less therapeutic. When you wrote to the Christians in Corinth you had to take them to task on a number of serious issues but first you gave sincere thanks for their special gifts.[3] It wasn't a matter of flattery but of recognising the genuinely good things about the people to whom you were writing, as well as the shortcomings which needed to be addressed.

If we have something negative which needs to be said it's usually possible to find a positive word of praise to put alongside it. Love leads us to do that for, as you said, 'love rejoices with the truth'.[4] Instead of the unholy glee which may come when we take someone apart with our criticism there can be the holy joy and satisfaction which comes when we build someone up in love.

Do you agree that motivation is what matters most? In a disagreement we might simply be out to put the other person down and justify ourselves. What we like to call principle may be no more than pride and prejudice. On the other hand, we may be anxious simply to contend for the truth, being less concerned about *who* is right than on upholding *what* is right.

Because human nature doesn't alter very much from one generation to the next, the issues you faced with regard to relationships seem much the same as those we face today. And the divinely inspired guidance you gave to your people applies equally to us nearly 2,000 years later.

You wrote to people in Ephesus: 'Make every effort to keep the unity of the Spirit through the bond of peace.'[5] That's an art which is not always easy to acquire. Maintaining the balance of grace and truth can be difficult but, God helping us, we continue to work at it.

Yours sincerely,

Wesley

[1]*Galatians 2:11;* [2]*Ephesians 4:15;* [3]*1 Corinthians 1:4-8;*
[4]*1 Corinthians 13:6b;* [5]*Ephesians 4:3*

46: A letter about 'accepting community'

Dear Paul,

IT seems you came from an honourable but narrowly sectarian background, being a Pharisee and a Hebrew of the Hebrews.[1] It's remarkable, then, that you became so accepting and inclusive. You said that in Christ there is neither Jew nor Greek, slave nor free, male nor female.[2] You affirmed that everyone who calls on the name of the Lord will be saved[3] and urged Christians to accept one another as Christ accepted them.[4]

But while you were so accepting of *people* you didn't find all kinds of *behaviour* acceptable within the Church. Where Christian conduct is concerned it can't be a case of 'anything goes'. For the good of all there are standards to be maintained. Evil must be kept at bay. In that sense the Church needs to be exclusive.

I've stood in what remains of the city of Corinth and thought about the heartache you had about at least one issue which arose there. The city was notorious for its licentiousness; it was a cesspool of immorality in which the church would have been submerged and lost without trace if the Christians had gone along with the local culture. You were shocked by a case of immorality in the congregation and perhaps even more disturbed that the leaders of the church – squeezed by the world into its own mould[5], no doubt – had been so accepting of what had taken place.[6] You felt it necessary to take a strong line. You said the man involved should be disciplined, not with a view to his breaking but to his ultimate making.

While in one sense the Church was to be an accepting community it could never be a permissive society. Christians had to dare to be different. However, I feel for you in those circumstances, for I know from experience how costly it can be to take a stand for what is right as a leader of God's people.

Sometimes the issues you faced were not so obviously black and white. For example, in Corinth the question also arose as to whether it was right to eat meat which had previously been offered to a pagan god. In one way there was nothing wrong with that, but you said that if the action caused someone else to stumble then it *was* wrong.[7] You placed great importance on maintaining a good example.

Today's generation has been called the 'me generation', with people acting on the belief that if something feels good it's alright. But pondering on your response to an issue which seems strange to us, I discover an important principle: we can't say we live to ourselves; we are all our brothers' or sisters' keepers. No doubt life was complicated in your time, but it's possibly even more so today.

Yours as always,

Wesley

[1]*Philippians 3:5;* [2]*Galatians 3:28;* [3]*Romans 10:13;* [4]*Romans 15:7;*
[5]*Romans 12:2 (J.B. Philips);* [6]*1 Corinthians 5:1-5;*
[7]*1 Corinthians 8:1-3*

47: A letter about blessings in disguise

Dear Paul,

SOME of the things which happened to you must have seemed like unmitigated disasters at the time. For example, it was no joke being placed under arrest by the Roman authorities. You must have thought your missionary activity, and perhaps even your life, was at an end. Then you discovered that what had happened to you was a blessing in disguise. You may recall writing to your much-loved friends in Philippi: 'Now I want you to know, brothers, that what has happened to me has really served to advance the gospel.'[1]

I understand that the word you used, translated here as 'advance', could relate to the progress of an army or an expedition and could also carry the thought of an advance party clearing away undergrowth or barriers which might impede the progress of the main force.

Surprisingly, you saw your imprisonment as serving that kind of purpose. You wrote: 'Because of my chains, most of the brothers in the Lord have been encouraged to speak the word of God more courageously.'[2] I recently visited the leader of a church who had just been told by his doctor that he probably didn't have long to live. Of course, the members of his congregation were greatly saddened, but, inspired by their leader's rock-solid faith and fortitude in the face of dire news, they redoubled their efforts to carry on the work for him as well as for the Lord. For them a tragedy became a testimony and an added incentive for service.

To meet a need I came out of retirement to give oversight to a number of centres of Christian witness. Praise the Lord, there was much to encourage me but there were also some concerns and I was again made aware of what you meant when you spoke of 'the care of the churches'. You may now be in a position to take in the wider picture of what is happening in the Church and to scan the history of the ways in which God has been making a path for the gospel through the centuries. Would you agree that revival may sometimes be a matter of seeing which way God is moving – and getting out of his way?

I fear that, sometimes, like thick undergrowth, our prejudices and entrenched ideas may block spiritual progress but clearing them away can be painful and seem disastrous. Our comfort zones may stand in the way of advance but we cherish them for all that. The way things have been is the way we would like them to remain. I greatly admire your vision and the way in which you engaged in positive 'possibility thinking'. You have been an example to Christian leaders through the years and you still are. I'm very grateful.

Yours sincerely,

Wesley

*Philippians 1:12; *Philippians 1:14*

48: A letter about saints

Dear Paul,

I'M not sure whether the word 'saint' has gone up or come down in the world. People are often quick to say they are *not* saints. In some branches of the Church it may take many years before a person is *officially* designated as one. As a result such people, although admirable, tend to seem remote and removed from ordinary people. With the greatest respect, I think you have seemed a bit that way yourself to some people, which is why in my letters to you I've tried to highlight some of your very human characteristics. I don't think you would have been displeased by that, for you certainly practised what you preached about taking a sober view of oneself.

You addressed one of your great letters to 'the saints' or 'the sanctified' at Corinth.[1] Did you have in mind only a few rare spirits in that place or were you thinking of the larger company of God's people? If it was the latter, many of 'the saints' or sanctified souls referred to were people on whom God still had a lot of work to do! There were problems in the congregation: the sort of things which sometimes occur in church groups today, sadly. Those people at Corinth were no plaster saints. They were scarcely the finished article when it came to holiness. In fact some seem to have given you quite a headache at times, yet didn't you still think of them as people set apart for God?

As a Jew you were brought up to think of the Temple and its sacrifices as specially marked out for God, and in a similar way as a Christian leader you taught that people should be holy temples or living sacrifices, dedicated to the Lord. You believed that ordinary people could be filled with the Spirit although still very human, possessing the treasure of truth while remaining earthen vessels. Holiness wasn't merely something for an elite class of spiritual supermen or superwomen who had 'arrived' spiritually. Those who were holy were always seeking to be more holy and reaching for higher altitudes of spiritual life. Is that right?

In church buildings today we sometimes see stained glass windows depicting saints. Some of them look rather wan and weary: pale, lifeless characters who are not a very good advertisement for the good life. By way of contrast I think of some Christians I know who are probably much more like the people you had in mind. Sure, they make mistakes sometimes and they certainly wouldn't claim to be the last word spiritually but they are saints alive for all that!

They are not at all ethereal. They often have rosy cheeks and laughing eyes. Almost invariably they have warm natures and the kind of love which seems to enfold other people in an accepting embrace. It's good to be with them. Without being overly pious or 'preachy' they make others want to be better men or women. In fact, they bear a strong resemblance to Jesus although they're probably quite unaware of that themselves.

And after all these years your letters still help in the making of people like that. That's wonderful!

Yours sincerely,

Wesley

¹1 Corinthians 1:2

49: A letter about women preaching

Dear Paul,

YOU'LL have gathered that I greatly appreciate your letters but you may not be surprised to know that some of your statements have led to a few arguments, increasingly so as times have changed and perceptions have altered through the years. Some people think you had a 'down' on women. On this assumption some have wondered whether as a young man you had a bad experience – like a broken marriage, for example – about which we know nothing. But that could well be impertinent and completely without foundation.

You were influenced by the culture and customs of your time. Like other Jewish boys in those days you were encouraged to give thanks that you were not born a woman or a Gentile! You were well aware that women took no part in synagogue services and although, as I believe, you were divinely inspired, you were also very human. As you put it, the treasure was in an earthen vessel. Often you were dealing with particular situations and sensitivities about which we know very little. Taking your words out of their local context could be misleading for us.

Writing to the sometimes troublesome Christians at Corinth you said women shouldn't speak in church,[1] but earlier in the same letter you said they shouldn't pray or prophesy *with their heads uncovered*[2] which, at the time, was considered immodest. Could it be that in the one instance you had in mind some inappropriate and contentious outspokenness while in the other it was about taking an acceptable part in religious exercises?

By the way, I should tell you that since your time many very holy women have been called to preach, and the Spirit has wonderfully blessed their ministry. It's even been said that some of the 'best men' in the Church have been women, although you might choke on that!

On the Day of Pentecost, Peter quoted the prophet Joel's words, 'your sons *and* daughters will prophesy'[3]. Your friend Dr Luke said that Phillip had no less than four daughters who had the gift of prophecy[4] without any apparent bother and you yourself certainly had lots of appreciation for the different contributions to church life of your 'fellow worker' Priscilla,[5] also Phoebe the deaconess[6] and others. You would surely agree you could hardly have got on without them.

In your first letter to Timothy you wrote about women in the church having authority over men, which was obviously a 'no-no' for many in your day[7] – and for a diminishing number today – although I have no difficulty with the idea myself. In your letter to the Galatians you said something which represented a spiritual breakthrough, although not everyone realised it at the time. You declared that in Christ there is neither male nor female; we are not all alike but in him we are all as one.[8] That was great! I would love to have discussed some of these matters with you personally and got them a bit clearer. One of the things I look forward to in Heaven is being able to get answers to a lot of questions which have puzzled me for years. If I can get near you for the crowds I will be grateful if you could spare me a little bit of time – or should I say eternity?

Yours hopefully,

Wesley

[1] *1 Corinthians 14:34;* [2] *1 Corinthians 11:5;* [3] *Acts 2:17;* [4] *Acts 21:9;* [5] *Acts 18:2 and Romans 16:3;* [6] *Romans 16:1;* [7] *1 Timothy 2:12;* [8] *Galatians 3:28*

50: A letter about music

Dear Paul,

AFTER reading and rereading your letters I feel I know you but there are times when I have to 'read between the lines' and make educated guesses. If I get it wrong, forgive me, but, for example, I have wondered to what extent you were into music.

I have grown up in a Christian tradition in which music plays a big part. Before I ever read a book on theology I learnt a lot from the songs I sang, as have friends of mine who, regretfully, have never read a book on Christian doctrine in their lives.

John Mark, your former personal assistant, wrote about the disciples of Jesus – and presumably the Lord himself – singing a hymn before going to the garden of Gethsemane.[1] What about you? I guess you must have done your share of singing. After all, you were brought up in a faith which had often been expressed in music and with a tradition of using brass, strings, percussion and anything else which could make a joyful noise to the Lord. The psalms you learnt in childhood were made for singing.

In your letter to the Colossians you gave a clear endorsement of music in the service of the soul when you wrote, 'Let the word of Christ dwell in you richly as you teach and admonish one another with all wisdom, and as you sing psalms, hymns and spiritual songs with gratitude in your hearts to God.'[2] I'm sure you practised what you preached and joined your voice with those of the converts in the various churches you visited.

Your dear friend, Dr Luke, left it on record that when you and Silas were imprisoned in Philippi you sang a duet at midnight.[3] I wonder what you sang? Was it 'Wake up, O sleeper, rise from the dead, and Christ will shine on you', which you quoted in your letter to the Ephesians?[4]

It's been suggested that in what we now identify as the second chapter of your letter to the church at Philippi you were actually quoting from a Christian hymn[5] – one of your own compositions, perhaps. Through the years Christianity has often been winged on its way by music and song and I'm glad to report that this is still happening. I'm not sure what you would make of some of the modern music but I fancy that you would say that if it's a vehicle for carrying the good news about Jesus then that's what matters most. Our personal musical taste may be beside the point.

By the way, you may be pleased to know that some of your own words have been set to music and sung by generations of 'Jesus people'. For example, one song begins, 'Fight the good fight' and another, 'Be strong in the grace of the Lord'. Then some years ago a piece written for brass bands had the title, *Portraits from St Paul's Epistles*. How about that?

Yours 'in Christ',

Wesley

[1]*Mark 14:26;* [2]*Colossians 3:16;* [3]*Acts 16:25;* [4]*Ephesians 5:14;* [5]*Philippians 2:5-11*

51: A letter about Aquila and Priscilla

Dear Paul,

IT'S a pity there's not a celestial postal service so I could get answers to all the questions I want to ask you. Apart from theological matters I'd like to know more about some of your friends. Sometimes there are only passing references to them in your letters, and not much more in Dr Luke's brief history of the Early Church.

Take Aquila and Priscilla for example, were they among the early converts in Rome or even among the visitors from that city who heard Peter preaching in Jerusalem on the Day of Pentecost? They were among those affected by the decree of the Emperor Claudius banishing Jews from the capital. I understand they moved to Corinth where you were busy planting a church.[1] Was there a street or district where tentmakers were concentrated? At any rate, because you shared that trade you met and it became possible for you to share work and accommodation, and, no doubt, some rich Christian fellowship. From Corinth the happy wanderers moved with you to Ephesus.[2] Then, eventually, they went back to Rome where the ban on Jews must apparently have been lifted.

Perusing your letters and Luke's account I notice that more often than not Priscilla's name is mentioned *before* that of her husband.[2,3] Was there significance in that? I've no problem with the principle of 'ladies before gentlemen' but wasn't it unusual to put it that way at that time? By way of explanation it's been suggested that Priscilla was a member of a distinguished Roman family. If that was so I'd love to know how this high-born woman came to meet and marry a Jewish artisan. Do I sense a hidden romance? If I was writing a religious novel based on this couple my imagination would run wild but I wish you were available to fill in the gaps in what we know and provide me with fact not fiction.

Priscilla and Aquila seem to be people who were always *giving*. For example, they gave hospitality. You speak of the church in their house – the church domestic, one might say – and no doubt you were glad to share their hospitality.[4] Apparently they also gave spiritual sustenance, particularly to a brilliant young man called Apollos[5] who was taken into their home and given a better understanding of the faith which he could then share with others. I'm afraid some older Christians can only criticise the younger generation but your friends did something better. Point taken!

You paid your friends a wonderful tribute when you wrote to their home congregation at Rome, 'They risked their lives for me.'[6] There must be a great story behind that sentence. You didn't elaborate but went on: 'Not only I but all the churches of the Gentiles are grateful to them.' You had lived and worked with them – wintered and summered them, as they say in some places – and you knew the secret of their loving lives. You said they were 'in Christ Jesus'.[7] That was what made them 'special'. If I may say so, it was what made you special also.

Yours sincerely,

Wesley

[1]*Acts 18:2;* [2]*Acts 18:18, 19;* [3]*Romans 16:3, 4; 2 Timothy 4:19;*
[4]*1 Corinthians 16:19;* [5]*Acts 18:26;* [6], [7]*Romans 16:3, 4*

52: A letter about friends and relationships

Dear Paul,

IT'S said a person's bare individuality is like the grit which gets into the oyster shell, and the pearl of life is made by the relationships we gather around us. Would you agree that your life was greatly enriched by some of the friends who supported you? I'm sure they gained even more from knowing you. If there's such a thing as 'sanctified envy' I have it when I think of those who received your shining words as they came freshly minted from your heart. Was it a deliberate strategy to attract not just followers but people who could themselves become leaders? (Anyone can see the pips in an apple but it takes special vision to see an apple in the pips!)

You certainly appear to have taken time to help such individuals develop their powers for the furtherance of the gospel. What's more, you were generous in giving them praise when praise was due. When it comes to appreciation, some people can't see beyond themselves, but you were not like that.

Timothy is a case in point. Did you think of him not so much as a colleague as a stand-in for the son you never had?[1] From the way you wrote, it seems like it, which is why we always tend to think of him as young, although presumably he got older like the rest of us. You saw he was 'stretchable material' so prepared him for leadership and then placed responsibility on his shoulders. He may have been naturally timid but writing to your friends in Philippi you said he had proved himself, because as a son with a father he had served with you in the work of the gospel.[2]

You spoke warmly about your travelling companion Luke, your 'dear friend' as you called him.[3] Wasn't it wonderful for you to have someone with you who was a physician, journalist and historian all rolled into one? A very handy combination! There's also a tradition that Luke was a painter, although whether he had much time to indulge that particular hobby while he was with you is open to doubt. Luke was the only non-Jew to write in what we call the New Testament and it's great to have his life of Jesus and his short history of the Early Church. He was certainly an excellent wordsmith.

Epaphroditus was another helper for whom you had appreciation. He had been sent by the Christians at Philippi, with a gift, to visit you on 'death row' and stay to give support. Wasn't that risky for him? I understand he fell ill and nearly died.[4] Did he fear that when he returned home some would think he had 'chickened out'? If so, the true position is made clear in your letter. He was your brother, your fellow worker and your fellow soldier as well as the messenger sent by his church. He had 'gambled' his life in order to be of service and should be welcomed home with honour.

I think greatness is revealed in the way a person treats those whom others regard as 'little people'. You certainly didn't take such people for granted. You had friends because you were a friend, as well as a great apostle.

Yours sincerely,

Wesley

*[1] 1 Timothy 1:18; [2]Philippians 2:22; [3]Colossians 4:14;
[4]Philippians 2:25-30*

105

53: A letter about Onesimus the runaway slave

Dear Paul,

WE never know how long anything we write may stay around. I once had to clear out office files which included some rather hasty letters written more than 50 years before. The writers could never have thought that what they had written would be perused so long afterwards.

Are you surprised that something from your voluminous private correspondence is still being read after nearly 2,000 years? I have in mind your little letter to Philemon[1], a solid citizen from Colossae who you led to Christ. He had a slave called Onesimus who absconded, probably with some stolen money to help him on the long journey to Rome.

There he found his way to where you were imprisoned at the time. You would have thought he would have given a wide berth to a situation where Roman guards could be found. A runaway slave was liable to be beaten, branded with a letter 'f' (standing for *fugitivus)* or even killed on capture. But perhaps he had heard his master speak glowingly about you so that, throwing caution to the winds, the lonely lad decided to look you up. Was it like that?

At any rate, you were able to lead the young fellow to Christ and in turn he was able to help you in some ways. I understand that his name meant 'profitable' and apparently he lived up to it so far as you were concerned although, if asked, his master might have taken a different view!

Was it while Onesimus was with you that, in your letters to the Ephesians and Colossians, you wrote about master/slave relationships?

At that stage, outright condemnation of slavery as such would have seemed like rebellion and brought swift retribution on the Church. But you sowed the seeds of eventual emancipation for all that. It seems you would have liked Onesimus to stay with you but the right thing was for him to return home and 'face the music' as the saying goes. However, you decided to give him a covering letter which is now in our Bible. You made it clear that although Onesimus was returning as a slave under Roman law he was also coming as a Christian and therefore as Philemon's brother in Christ. That suggestion would have made most slave masters gulp but you knew your man and could remind him that anyway he owed you something spiritually.

You offered to pay any debts your young friend may have incurred. I hope I'm not impertinent, but that makes me think you must have had some private financial means.

According to your friend Luke, Felix the Roman governor must have had the same idea for he thought you could afford to pay a bribe[2]. But for the passage of years I wouldn't dare to pry but now I wonder whether, despite the fact that you became a Christian, you received some share of your family's estate?

We don't know the result of your appeal to Philemon and the other Christians who used to meet in his house. I would like to feel that on your recommendation Onesimus was forgiven and perhaps eventually set free. Years later a collection of your letters was made, probably in Ephesus. And at the time the bishop in that city was called Onesimus. Could he have been the former runaway slave for whom the little letter written on his behalf might have been most precious of them all? I don't know; I just wonder.

Yours sincerely,

Wesley

[1]*Philemon;* [2]*Acts 24:26*

107

54: A letter about the secretary

Dear Paul,

I THINK, like me, you had good reason to be grateful for private secretaries who helped you with your correspondence. I remember on one occasion feeling pleased with myself and remarking that I had written 50 letters that day. My hard working secretary looked up at me with what I imagined was wonderment in her eyes and then remarked, 'It's amazing what one man can accomplish – when he doesn't have to do the work himself!' Of course, she was right.

No disrespect to you, Paul, but I don't think being your secretary would have been easy. Your inspired thoughts were sometimes complicated and your words came in cascades. The sentences were long and convoluted on occasion; sometimes they never seem to finish. Always you would have seen the people beyond the papyrus. Your burning heart and your active mind longed to reach across the miles. Communication was the essence of your work, and compared with the facilities of today the means at your disposal were limited. It was often a matter of finding someone who would deliver a scroll by hand.

I picture you in a small room or prison cell, pacing up and down as you pour out your concern for a particular church and its needs. And there, crouched over a low table, is the long-suffering secretary ready to tear his hair as his pen sputters as he tries to keep up with your inspired flow of words. It is a matter of conjecture how much your secretaries affected the shape and style of your letters. Almost certainly we owe them a great debt for their painstaking work behind the scenes.

As a rule you added a signature and perhaps a brief greeting to your letters as a sign of authenticity, but at the end of your passionate letter to the Galatians you added a whole paragraph, writing in large letters.[1] Did you write like that because you had a problem with your eyesight? Or was it so your friends could read your words without difficulty, even by the flickering light of candles?

Generally, your secretaries remained anonymous. Their names are known to God but not to us. However, Tertius included his name and greetings in your letter to the church at Rome.[2] Am I right in thinking that when you wrote you were enjoying excellent hospitality in the home of a wealthy Christian in Corinth called Gaius[2], and that there you had plenty of time to craft your fullest exposition of the faith? In that monumental work your secretary played an important part, as you would agree. For that reason I'm sure you wouldn't have begrudged him the opportunity to send a brief word to Christians in Rome with whom he may have had previous contacts.

I'm confident that you didn't look down on people who looked up to you. I mean, you would have appreciated the support given by those whose faithfulness helped you leave a legacy of thought which still enriches us today. We salute them too.

Yours sincerely,

Wesley

[1]Galatians 6:11; [2]Romans 16:22, 23

55: A letter about backsliding

Dear Paul,

IT seems, like me, you couldn't always pick winners. Some of your chosen colleagues let you down badly which given the frailties of human nature may not be surprising. But it would still have been very hurtful when people in whom you had placed confidence fell by the wayside.

I've been thinking about Demas. We know nothing about him apart from what can be deduced from the three brief mentions you give him in your dispatches. However, I fancy I could plot his spiritual graph from those references, and the downward trend is all too familiar.

In the note you sent to Philemon you describe Demas as your 'fellow worker'[1] not your subordinate or your underling. His stock seems high at this point. I would have been mightily pleased to be described in such a way. You were a prominent leader of the Church yet you didn't patronise the young recruit. Rather you treated him as an equal because you saw potential in him.

It's a mark of a good leader to be able to attract not just followers but potential leaders. You did that in many cases. But Demas was a disappointment. When you wrote to the Christians at Colossae your reference was only a passing '... and Demas'[2]. Perhaps I shouldn't presume to read your unspoken thoughts but I've wondered whether you may have come to have an uncomfortable feeling about the young man. Perhaps you couldn't put your finger on anything specific. He may have been continuing to give service but did you sense this was becoming mechanical and that some of the early glow had gone?

110

At all events, those fears proved well-founded. You were in prison awaiting execution when you wrote to Timothy: 'Demas, because he loved this world, has deserted me and has gone to Thessalonica.'[3] Was there a sob in your voice when you said those words? No doubt, like other backsliders, the young man had some excuse for packing his bags and leaving you in your hour of need but you gave the real reason: worldliness.

Would you agree that endurance often breaks not from over-strain but from under-motivation? Was that the problem with Demas? There's a tradition, which may or may not be true, that after leaving you the young man took a job swinging incense before an idol in a heathen temple. What a come-down that would have been from the high calling which had been his in Christ!

Not even across the centuries would I be judgmental of Demas. But for the grace of God I might have gone the same way. Why, even you recognised the danger of becoming disqualified. I've no doubt your prayers followed Demas and any others who fell from grace, even as my prayers follow people in these days. I can certainly share your feelings.

Yours faithfully

Wesley

[1]Philemon 23, 24; [2]Colossians 4:14; [3]2 Timothy 4:10

56: A letter about finding Christians in unlikely places

Dear Paul,

'SERENDIPITY' describes the faculty for making happy and unexpected discoveries. You wouldn't have known the word but I'm sure you had the gift. For example, you would have been thrilled, and perhaps surprised, to find Christians in quite unexpected places. I've had that experience. I recall contact with some parliamentarians who, regardless of party differences, met regularly for prayer. I remember people who had found Christ in prison. And my heart has been gladdened to discover Christian fellowship between people in showbusiness, in the police and among athletes. I've found that the network of grace is more extensive than I thought. Sometimes it's underground and sometimes not, sometimes organised in a formal way and sometimes not.

At times you might have felt very much alone, like the prophet Elijah at one point. Then, like him, you discovered many others shared your faith and you were 'surprised by joy' as a result. There's a phrase in your letter to the Christians at Philippi which seems to point to something like that. You write: 'All the saints send you greetings, especially those who belong to Caesar's household.'[1] I'd like to ask you about some of those who were part of 'the royal household' *and* the household of faith. Some of their stories would make fascinating reading, I'm sure.

You were writing from Rome where you had to wait a long time for a date to be set for your trial. As the capital of the Roman

112

Empire, Rome was the centre of what we would now describe as the civil service, a place where bureaucracy flourished. Did those you described as being of Caesar's household include secretaries, financial controllers and government administrators as well as servants in the imperial palace?

Some may have been slaves in lowly positions but did you discover secret disciples or sympathisers who were high officials? A man to whom your friend Luke seems to have prudently given the pseudonym 'Theophilus' may have been one such and it's amazing that Christianity so quickly penetrated the higher ranks of officialdom. We know there were people from Rome present in Jerusalem on the Day of Pentecost. Did they take back the good news to the heart of the empire and form the nucleus of the church there? And were they among your visitors, possibly clandestine, while you were under house arrest?

It seems that Philippi was a colony largely populated by army veterans and other Roman citizens, perhaps including civil servants. It would therefore have been natural if some of those with whom you had contact in the capital wanted to send greetings to Christian colleagues they knew in Philippi. I believe that, as in your day, God often has his 'secret agents' strategically placed for our encouragement. I try to look out for them because sometimes they are angels of mercy just when I need them. By the same token, I want to be in the right place at the right time for others who may need encouragement through the network.

Yours sincerely,

Wesley

'Philippians 4:22

113

57: A letter about Barnabas

Dear Paul,

CONTEMPLATING your God-blessed life and ministry naturally brings into focus some of your associates. For example, I notice that the name of your old colleague Barnabas means 'the son of encouragement'.[1] He certainly lived up to his name. After your conversion some of the Christians in Jerusalem were sceptical about your motives and who could blame them after the way you had persecuted the Church? But Barnabas believed the best and encouraged you.[2] Perhaps, without his backing, Saul of Tarsus might not have become Paul the Apostle. Or is that an overstatement?

When a lot of non-Jews became Christians in Antioch it was Barnabas who rescued you from obscurity in your home city of Tarsus so you could give instruction to the new converts.[3] Do you agree it was his encouragement that led you to 'centre stage' and a pivotal role in the development of the Early Church? Dr Luke described Barnabas as a good man, full of the Holy Spirit and faith, and doubtless you agreed with that description. You noted also that, like you, he could turn his hand to practical work in order to support himself.

Barnabas accompanied you on your first missionary journey, which began with a visit to his native Cyprus. I was there a while ago and recalled the work you did in that place. Young John Mark, a cousin of Barnabas, also went with you as a helper but seems to have got homesick and gone home to his mother in Jerusalem.[4] Am I right in thinking you were infuriated by that? Did you think Mark was a spiritual wimp? At any rate, when cousin Barnabas wanted to give the boy another chance and take him on a second missionary journey[5] with you there was quite a barney[6] – if the pun may be pardoned. You might prefer to forget that altercation but good came out of it in that while Barnabas and John Mark went evangelising in one direction you and Silas went in another. Was it out of loyalty to you that Luke didn't mention Barnabas after that? But you appear not to have held any resentment, for while you and Barnabas didn't pair up again you gave him honourable mention in some of your letters.[7] Even more significantly, John Mark must have rehabilitated himself in your affections because later – perhaps after the death of Barnabas – you regarded him as one of your most faithful helpers.[8]

You told the Christians in Thessalonica to encourage one another[9] and I wonder whether at the back of your mind you had the memory of Barnabas who gave you encouragement just when you needed it. We can't all hit headlines or do spectacular things for God but the ministry of encouragement can often prove a spiritual lifesaver. It's sad that so many converts who come through the front door of the church disappear as backsliders through the rear door. If the congregation was more of a community of encouragement, perhaps the sad loss could be avoided. Barnabas could give us the cue we need. What do you think?

Yours sincerely,

Wesley

[1]Acts 4:36; [2]Acts 9:27; [3]Acts 11:25; [4]Acts 13:13; [5]Acts 15:37, 38; [6]Acts 15:39-41; [7]Galatians 2:9; [8]Colossians 4:10; [9]1 Thessalonians 4:18

58: A letter about slavery

Dear Paul,

IN previous letters I've raised some matters you wrote about but I also wonder about some things you didn't write about, at least, not in the letters which have survived. For example, why did you – and indeed our Lord himself - not come out strongly against slavery?

Two out of three of everyone on the streets of Rome were slaves. Some were well treated and had considerable responsibility but for others it was a different story. They could be beaten, branded and even killed with few questions asked. They were merely their master's goods and chattels, often regarded as less than human. Some Christian leaders who followed you denounced this but you didn't. I wonder why.

Of course, slavery was an institution largely taken for granted in your day. Did you sense it was not the time to make a frontal attack on something so much part of society? Such an attack would certainly have brought sharp reaction from those with vested interests, including the Roman authorities. Then, if the Lord was to make an early return, as at one time you expected, the whole issue would be overtaken by that great event anyway. Was that in your mind? Should we conclude that while for some people in some situations it's right to speak out openly against unjust institutions, there may be times when it's better to put the gospel to work quietly, like yeast, and ultimately bring about change in that way?

While you didn't overtly attack the institution of slavery I note you had plenty to say about how to behave within it.[1] While slaves were to labour conscientiously for an earthly master they were to remember that they also laboured for a Heavenly Master. The masters were to be kindly and realise they too were responsible to God. The degradation of the slave and the pride of the master should be abolished by the gospel. Class distinction was a 'no no'. I have written separately about that little note you sent to Philemon about his runaway slave Onesimus in which you said he should be received back not only as a slave but as a dear brother. That was a 'big ask', given the climate at the time.

You made it clear that social distinctions could and should be transcended by spiritual relationships. In Christ the slave and the free man were as one.[2] What was more, even though you were proud of your freedom as a citizen of Rome, you wrote to Christians in the capital of the empire that you were a willing slave of the Lord Jesus. That was really something.

Very sincerely yours,

Wesley

[1]Colossians 3:22-4:1; [2]Galatians 3:28

59: A letter about stewardship

Dear Paul,

I GUESS, like me, you had all sorts of hospitality offered to you in the course of your travels – some good and some not so special. There would have been times when you 'did it tough', as the saying goes, and others when, staying in the home of someone rich, like Gaius at Corinth for example, you had every comfort.

In wealthy homes you would have seen the importance of the role of the steward or *oikonomos* (to use the Greek term, from which our English word 'economy' is derived). He was a man who could make all the difference to the running of a household, ordering the supplies and taking on slaves to do the chores. The *oikonomos*, even as a slave, had great authority and was expected to manage the whole estate efficiently – or else!

At the end of the day, though, he didn't own what he administered. He was a man under authority, responsible to his master. Something of this must have been in your mind when you wrote to the church in Corinth and, thinking of your own stewardship, declared: 'It is required that those who have been given a trust must prove faithful.'[1]

In the Early Church you had great prestige and authority, yet you called yourself a slave of Christ. You knew the Church and its message was only yours in trust; you were an *oikonomos* or steward, accountable to God. I guess you were familiar with the principle of stewardship from your youth. It was something as large as life and as wide as the world. You knew the earth was the Lord's[2] and the cattle upon a thousand hills were his[3] and you were taught that Adam and Eve had been given stewardship of the earth[4].

Would you agree that we humans have often forgotten that with all our privileges we are not owners but stewards or managers, God's housekeepers one might say, and accountable for our actions? We've sometimes squandered the earth's resources, perverted knowledge and lived in luxury while others have starved. That must have been true in your day but I think it is even more the case today. I'm sorry to say we live in what has been called the 'me generation' with great emphasis on human rights but less concern about corresponding responsibilities. As a result of human selfishness the state of our environment is now suffering in a big way.

Jesus was the only perfect Steward who ever lived and we need to see our stewardship in the light of the Cross. Our Lord could say he had completed the work God gave him to do; he was faithful to the end. You also could say that you had kept the faith and finished the race, and I would like to be able to say the same one day. It's said the world crowns success but God crowns faithfulness, and I fancy you are in a position to confirm that.

Yours faithfully,

Wesley

[1] *1 Corinthians 4:2;* [2] *Psalm 24:1;* [3] *Psalm 50:10;* [4] *Genesis 1:28*

119

60: A letter about doing no harm to others

Dear Paul,

SOME of the issues which trouble modern Christians were unknown in your time, just as some of the problems you faced no longer arise. Yet there are principles which you were inspired to lay down which can still apply although circumstances are different.

In your day a lot of meat was offered to idols in pagan temples. Part of the carcass was placed on the altar as a sacrifice to be consumed by fire. Some portions were given to the officiating priest and the rest went back to the person making the offering. I guess it would have been clear that Christians should not take part in religious feasts in pagan temples but the grey area would have to do with meat which had been offered before an idol and then found its way to a market where it was sold for consumption in private homes.

Some of your friends took the view that there was no harm in eating the meat because the pagan gods did not really exist anyway. But others felt that *when it was known* that meat had been part of an offering, to eat it was to compromise a person's Christian commitment.

So you laid down the principle that even to do something which was harmless in itself would be wrong if the action could be a stumbling block to others. It may be better to limit our liberty for the sake of our example, for no one is an island. As Christians we are each our brother's (or sister's) keeper and we need to be careful that we don't contribute to someone else's downfall.

Regarding the issue of meat offered to idols, you wrote to your friends in Corinth: 'If what I eat causes my brother to fall into sin, I will never eat meat again.'[1]

There may have been places to which you could have gone, and things you might have done, without suffering any spiritual harm yourself, but you always kept in mind the possible effect on weaker souls. To use an old-fashioned term, you, as a leader, tried to walk circumspectly, conscious that people might follow you to their harm instead of to their good.

I recall the example of a Christian minister who was given to drinking alcohol, although not to excess. A youth in his congregation followed his example and subsequently plumbed the depths as an alcoholic. Asked what had led to his downfall, he said he had seen his minister imbibing and thought there could be no harm if he did the same. Unfortunately, for him the story was very different.

I'm very conscious of my faults and the need to seek for grace, not only for my own sake but for that of others who might look to me for an example. People mark the way we Christians conduct ourselves. They notice not just our actions but our reactions and what we say and do in our unguarded moments. That would be an intolerable burden upon us but for the promised presence and support of the Holy Spirit, as I think you would agree.

Yours sincerely,

Wesley

[1] *1 Corinthians 8:1-13*

61: A letter about the therapy of thanksgiving

Dear Paul,

WHEN I was a child I was taught to say 'thank you' for any gift or service I received. I wonder if it was the same with you. Certainly, you were not slow to express appreciation to those who helped you in your ministry and, especially, to give thanks to God.

In your writings to some of the churches you emphasised the grace of gratitude. For example, you not only told the Christians at Thessalonica that it was God's will for them to be sanctified but also that God willed that they should give thanks *in all circumstances*[1] – which may have seemed a tall order. So I reckon you thought that thankfulness was an essential part of holiness. Is that right?

Not as often as I should, I sometimes express gratitude in advance, in anticipation of blessings yet to be received. That takes faith and I'm not always as strong in that department as I should be. In fact, I sometimes have not only a fight *of* faith but a fight *for* faith as well, if you understand what I mean.

Reading between the lines of your letters I sense that, like most people, you had your 'down' times but I'm sure you discovered the therapy of thanksgiving. Can I share with you that if I am having a bad day I often exercise my body and soul by going for a walk, determined that, from the time I leave my home to the time I return, I will maintain a constant stream of thanksgiving to God. I give thanks for the flowers, the trees, the birds, the children I meet along the way, and so on. When I first tried this I thought I'd run out of reasons for thanksgiving but I've never done so. One thing leads to another and even if I leave home feeling a bit of a grouch, I return knowing God is good and his blessings more than I can count. I wouldn't be surprised if you did the same kind of thing as you trudged along the dusty roads. A thankful heart would have lightened your steps.

In one translation of your letter to the Colossians I came across a sentence which gave a fillip to my prayer life. You were translated as saying: 'Maintain your zest for prayer by thanksgiving.'[2] Sometimes my praying has lacked zest because it has consisted of repetitions and sometimes selfish requests. But when I make a point of including plenty of praise and thanksgiving my prayers seem to take wings.

Would you agree that one of the main reasons for a lack of thanksgiving is thoughtlessness? It's possible to take many good things for granted – until they are taken from us. Then we realise how blessed we have been. But if we think, we will surely find reason to thank!

Yours thankfully,

Wesley

[1] 1 Thessalonians 5:18; [2] Colossians 4:2

123

62: A letter about real love

Dear Paul,

WHILE tradition has it that your friend Luke was an artist there's no hint that you ever worked with a palette and brush, but you were certainly an artist in your use of words. For example, when writing to the Corinthians you penned what we now call 'the love chapter'[1]. You sought to describe the supreme gift but in fact you also described the Giver. Was it without realising it that you painted a portrait of Jesus, the one in whom love was perfectly expressed?

Sometimes in my reading I have taken the liberty of substituting the name Jesus for the word love and have found the passage has been personalised in a wonderful way. At first you seem to have sketched in a contrasting background by mentioning some of the things which those to whom you were writing might have regarded highly, such as an ability to speak in strange tongues, to prophesy, to fathom mysteries, give to charity or even suffer martyrdom. You made plain that without love those things are like shadows without form or substance, so you push them into the background.

Then you went on to describe some of the things which characterise the special kind of love you had in mind and which were in fact features in the life of our Lord. You highlighted *patience* and *kindness* and I wonder whether in your mind you pictured Jesus with his sometimes faithless disciples, or pictured him finding time for lively children or reaching out to a needy widow. You wrote about *not envying or being proud or rude* and the picture conjured up was of the One you had come to know by faith, the 'Christ of experience' who was your daily companion. In another place you wrote about having the attitude of Christ[2] and I believe his thinking had permeated yours, perhaps more than you realised.

You continued: 'It [love] is not self-seeking, it is not easily angered, it keeps no record of wrongs. Love does not delight in evil but rejoices with the truth. It always protects, always trusts, always hopes, always perseveres.'[3] All of that was Jesus to a 'T'. You were a man in Christ, 'wrapped up in him', so very naturally the ideals you projected were coloured by your communion with the Lord; his face was the one most often on the screen of your mind.

You said the great thing about love is that it lasts. The values of Jesus are enduring, and that's a comfort to those of us who live in changing times. Many things which we thought were solid have been swept away. Much that was once accepted behaviour has gone by the board and is derided as 'old fashioned'. Even the word love has been debased and devalued but the special kind of love which you described and which Jesus exemplified is never outmoded. We can stake our lives on that.

Your colleague the Apostle John is often thought of as the 'apostle of love' while you're remembered for your powerful emphasis on 'justification by faith'. Yet you knew that love is even greater than faith, as the end is greater than the means. So you wrote: 'Now these three remain: faith, hope and love. But the greatest of these is love.'[4] Real love is indeed the greatest thing in the world and what the human race needs most of all.

Yours in the love of Christ,

Wesley

[1] *1 Corinthians 13:1-13;* [2] *Philippians 2:5;* [3] *1 Corinthians 13:5b-7;* [4] *verse 13*

125

63: A letter about divine discontent

Dear Paul,

IN some parts of the world there is more affluence than ever before. Many people have 'never had it so good'. Yet I'm not sure there is a great increase in contentment. The more some people have, the more they want. You wrote to your friends in Philippi: 'I have learned to be content whatever the circumstances'[1] but seeing you were in prison at the time I conclude that your wealth must have been in the fewness of your wants rather than in many material possessions. It also seems that contentment was something you learned, an acquired art rather than an innate characteristic.

Obviously contentment is a good thing but I'm dubious about it in some forms and in some people. Contentment can be confused with complacency. I know in some respects you had a divine discontent with the status quo and strained every nerve to change things for the better. Christians are among those who through the centuries have sought to right wrongs and make the world a better place. Those who fought to eliminate slavery are a case in point and the world is better for their constructive discontent.

It seems you learned to accept your own lot and see it in the larger context of God's providential care. You wrote: 'I know what it is to be in need, and I know what it is to have plenty. I have learned the secret of being content in any and every situation, whether well fed or hungry, whether living in plenty or in want. I can do everything through him who gives me strength.'[2]

126

I don't think you deliberately sought privation, or wanted to wear a hair shirt, for that would have been unhealthy. You appealed to higher Roman authority when you felt you were being treated wrongly. You saw possible release from prison as good for you and those you sought to serve. But if that didn't happen, you believed God could turn a negative into a positive experience and use it for the advance of the gospel. Having done your best you were content to leave the rest with God. You believed that in everything he would undertake and overrule. You were convinced that you were not outside his providential care and you had enough faith to be ready to place yourself in his hands.

Sometimes, in my own experience, destructive discontent has arisen because of a lack of simple trust in God. For some people, faith seems to come easily but it's not always been like that for me. Faith is a gift in itself as well as the means by which we receive other gifts from God and I often pray for more of the 'trust that brings the triumph'.[3] Perhaps at times you felt the need to pray along similar lines, so will understand the failures of some of us who are still trying to finish the Christian race. Like most people I'm more ready to follow footsteps than advice and I'm trying to follow your example and walk as you walked, by the grace of God.

Yours sincerely,

Wesley

Philippians 4:11b; [2]Philippians 4:12, 13; [3]SASB 213 v 3

127

64: A letter about 'redeeming the time'

Dear Paul,

YOU'D be amazed at the number of so-called time-saving devices around these days. The trouble is, people don't seem to know what happens to the time saved! Thanks to medical science, people are living longer than ever but they still say they're short of time. Could it be that we waste more time than we realise? I read a survey which claimed the average person spends 16 hours a year looking for their keys, simply because they don't have a place for everything and everything in its place.

I suspect things were the same in your day. I imagine you got exasperated if you saw people – especially Christians – not making the best use of the golden hours and jewelled moments at their disposal. You told the people at Ephesus they should make the most of every opportunity[1] to do good, 'redeeming the time' available to them. They should not only work hard but 'work smart' for the furtherance of the gospel,

I'm sure you practised what you preached. From your youth you knew the words of the psalmist: 'Teach us to number our days aright that we may gain a heart of wisdom'[2] and when you became a Christian this must have seemed more imperative than ever, for you felt the time was short and the Lord was at hand. Sometimes we think of blocks of time but in fact the future, like the past, is only a series of 'nows' which is why I'm sure you were acutely aware of what's been called 'the sacrament of the present moment'.

128

You must have wanted to dedicate every minute to the high and holy task which was yours, yet I don't think you lived under the tyranny of time. You didn't become frantic in your service. With all your zealous effort you could still write: 'the peace of God which transcends all understanding, will guard your hearts and your minds in Christ Jesus'.[3] Was that because you took time out to wait on the Lord and recharge your energies without feeling guilty about it? That kind of balance is important. Sometimes I manage to achieve it but not always.

Jesus taught that we should live in 'day tight' compartments, not fretting over the past or fearing the future but making the most of the present.[4]

It might help if we sometimes conducted an audit of our use of time and made a brief note of the way we spend the hours of a day. We might both surprise ourselves and profit from the experience. You said Christians should examine themselves, and perhaps this is one way of doing so. Then, having established our priorities and worked out what should and what should not be kept in our daily programme, we could offer our time to God knowing that in return he will give us eternity. That's right, isn't it?

Yours sincerely,

Wesley

[1]*Ephesians 5:16;* [2]*Psalm 90:12;* [3]*Philippians 4:7;* [4]*Matthew 6:34*

129

65: A letter about hope

Dear Paul,

A FELLOW countryman of yours who spent time in a harsh prison camp wondered why some prisoners survived while others did not. He came to the conclusion that the most important factor was a vision for the future, or, in other words, hope. Some people naturally possess a sanguine temperament. They cheerfully hope for the best while others fear the worst. Looking on the bright side is almost second nature in their case. Good for them! Whether that would describe you, I'm not sure. At any rate, I think you possessed something more than apostolic optimism, good as that might have been.

You rated hope, along with faith and love, as of great worth. Like oxygen in the lungs, it was what kept you going mentally and spiritually. In the Hebrew Scriptures which form what we now call the Old Testament, hope was largely limited to life on earth, and you cherished that. You hoped to travel to new places and make more converts. There was the anticipation of revisiting churches you had already founded and strengthening believers in the most holy faith. But for you there was much more. You wrote to Christians in Corinth: 'If only for this life we have hope in Christ, we are to be pitied more than all men.'[1]

It seems you had ever higher hopes. In fact they knew no limits. You looked for the second coming of Jesus – in God's own time – and beyond that, a life of blessedness in Heaven. So, as the saying goes, 'How come?' The clue may be in something you wrote to the Roman church: 'Hope does not disappoint us, because God has poured out his love into our hearts by the Holy Spirit.'[2]

For us – as it could have been for you at times – life sometimes seems grim. We find ourselves up against it in one way or another. But there are no hopeless situations, just people in them who have lost hope and are therefore ready to 'put down their bundle'. Unfortunately, there are plenty of people like that about. There is no light in their eyes, no glow of anticipation on their cheeks. They're going nowhere and they know it.

For you, hope was the gift of a loving Heavenly Father who would not lead you on with false promises then leave you to languish in despair.

Don't you think God must be hopeful by nature otherwise he would have given up on this world long ago? I believe that through grace he will give us something of what he is by nature. He doesn't want our lives to be shrouded in gloom or plagued by doubt. We were not meant to grope our way through the darkness of our times. You wrote to your Roman friends, 'May the God of hope fill you with all joy and peace as you trust in him, so that you may overflow with hope by the power of the Holy Spirit.' [3] If you don't mind, I'm going to take those words for myself.

Yours sincerely,

Wesley

[1] 1 Corinthians 15:19; [2] Romans 5:5; [3] Romans 15:13

131

66: A letter about the 'phantom pain' of past sin

Dear Paul,

ISN'T it wonderful to know we've been forgiven and don't need to carry a burden of guilt any more? I imagine you might have felt bowed down with remorse about the way in which you persecuted the early Church. Did you meet people whose relatives had suffered because of you? Recriminations would have been hard to take. Memories might have been crippling. But you could testify that God had forgiven you. What relief and release that must have brought! The past had been dealt with. You had God's word on that.

You wrote to Christians at Colossae: 'He has rescued us from the dominion of darkness and brought us into the kingdom of the Son he loves, in whom we have redemption, the forgiveness of sins.'[1] The trouble with a lot of Christians is that they don't *feel* forgiven. God has been gracious enough to pardon them. They're debt free. But you wouldn't think so. Guilt is written all over their faces. The night hours are still disturbed with thoughts of what might have been and the feeling that they must struggle and strain to settle their account with Heaven – as if that were humanly possible.

You had a special concern for people who thought salvation came through works rather than by faith and by simply accepting that God, for Jesus' sake, accepted them. From many years of experience in pastoral care I know that problem is still around. I understand that after a surgeon has removed a diseased limb the patient may continue to feel phantom pain even though the

132

original cause has been taken away. Perhaps the same applies in a spiritual sense. In accordance with his Word, God has removed our transgressions from us but we don't always have the faith to know and feel this is so.

Do you think it's because we don't fully realise how gracious God has been in forgiving us that we're sometimes not ready to forgive when we're injured by someone else? Our Lord spoke of a man who was pardoned for an enormous debt then dealt harshly with someone who owed him a trivial amount[2]. We can be like that at times. Could it be because the glory of being forgiven hasn't really changed our hearts and made them more open to others?

When we really latch on to the truth of the amazing grace of God it will not only make us more gracious towards other people but take a lot of the stress out of our lives. Having proved that God loves us, what else have we to prove? The past can't be relived but it can be outlived, by the grace of God. Your own spirit was liberated so that you could write to your friends in Philippi: 'Forgetting what is behind and straining towards what is ahead, I press on towards the goal to win the prize for which God has called me heavenwards in Christ Jesus.'[3]

I'm right behind you!

Yours sincerely,

Wesley

[1]Colossians 1:13, 14; [2]Matthew 18:28-35; [3]Philippians 3:13b, 14

67: A letter about peace with God

Dear Paul,

THROUGH visiting Israel I have become familiar with the common Hebrew greeting, *Shalom!* – meaning peace. I believe the word is rich in meaning and can indicate not only a cessation of hostilities but wholeness, soundness, health, prosperity. It must often have been on your lips but, I wonder, did frequent use turn it into a cliché rather like 'Good day' in English? Was a beautiful word employed rather thoughtlessly at times?

In that case did the term take on new meaning for you after you became a Christian and discovered how the Lord was in the habit of bestowing the blessing of *his* peace upon the disciples? I recall a wealthy woman who told me she would give all she possessed to find peace of heart. You must have met people with a similar yearning. Indeed you must have felt it yourself – which might be why, in your writings which have survived, you made more than 40 references to peace. Through the Holy Spirit the Lord spoke words of peace to your turbulent spirit, as at times he has spoken to my own heart.

To your friends at Philippi you wrote about the peace *of* God: 'The peace of God which transcends all understanding, will guard your hearts and your minds in Christ Jesus.'[1] You felt that something which was of the very nature of God could be like a sentinel of the soul. Seeing you were writing from prison, was your turn of phrase inspired by the sight of your Roman guard? I'm sure you wrote out of personal experience, as you did when, writing to the Romans, you described the experience of peace *with* God: 'We have peace with God through our Lord Jesus Christ.'[2] There had

134

been a time when, despite your religious zeal, you actually fought against God, but then peace was declared and reconciliation took place. Thereafter you fought for God, not against him

You realised the importance of having peace not only in your vertical relationship with God but also in horizontal ones with other people. You wrote to Rome: 'If it is possible, as far as it depends on you, live at peace with everyone.'[3] Reading between the lines I sense you knew this was a tall order. Sometimes peace may depend on others as well as on us, but I'm sure you found that determined friendliness can often break through seemingly insurmountable barriers.

Our Lord's blessing was not on mere peace lovers but on *peace makers,* on those who create an atmosphere of acceptance in place of antagonism. That is hard work but good work, as I'm sure you would agree. True peace is not merely the absence of war but the presence of love. Describing some leaders of his day the prophet Jeremiah declared: '"Peace, peace," they say, when there is no peace.'[4] I'm afraid that could also be said about some in these days although not all, thank God.

Now I must close. *Shalom!*

Yours sincerely,

Wesley

[1]*Philippians 4:7;* [2]*Romans 5:1;* [3]*Romans 12:18;* [4]*Jeremiah 6:14*

68: A letter about accepting others in love

Dear Paul,

WE live in a very divided world with many people refusing to accept others, not because of anything they have said or done but just because they are of a different race, religion, colour or gender. With our modern means of communication we're almost overwhelmed with news of tension in various parts of the world. In some cases this has led to massacres of men, women and children on a huge scale. It has been terrible, but do I hear you asking 'What's new?'

Wasn't the atmosphere in which you grew up also polluted by discrimination, with – for example – undying hostility between your own race and neighbouring people of different ethnic origin? Didn't Jews tend to despise Gentiles, and wasn't that reciprocal? I get the impression that, as a Jew called to be an apostle to the Gentiles, you had to contend with discrimination in your converts and perhaps, in some ways, even within your own heart and mind. You raised the standard about everyone being one in Christ but I suspect that, like many of us, you didn't always find it easy to live up to the standard you proclaimed. It's remarkable that by grace you overcame ingrained prejudices in the way you did.

You wrote to the church in Rome: 'Accept one another, then, just as Christ accepted you, in order to bring praise to God.'[1] Accepting some people is not difficult. They don't 'rub us up the wrong way'. They have sensible views and nice manners. In fact they're rather like us! On the other hand there are people who get on our nerves.

We have an instinctive dislike for them, either because they're very different from us or, possibly, because we see in them traits we refuse to recognise in ourselves. But clearly you believed we should accept and love even those we don't naturally like, and sometimes that's a tall order.

We might not approve of what people do. We might not go along with their beliefs. We might not accept their lifestyle as being what it ought to be. But you made it clear that we should still accept *them* as people, made in the likeness of God. We should try to be better not bitter.

The example you held up was that of Jesus. He accepted people, where they were, for what they were and for what they might become. Writing to your friends in Rome you made it clear that God graciously accepts people.[2] It is for us, by faith, to accept his acceptance and then, in a similar way, be accepting of other people. Discrimination brings God into disrepute. When people hear of violent conflict between people of different faiths they sometimes say: 'If that's religion, I want nothing to do with it.' But when, while remaining true to ourselves and our beliefs, we can accept other people in love then we bring praise to God. I think that's the sense of what you wrote. It certainly makes sense to me.

Yours sincerely,

Wesley

[1]Romans 15:7; [2]Romans 14:3

137

69: A letter about the blessing of being able both to remember and forget

Dear Paul,

AS we get older we can become absent-minded and have what are euphemistically described as 'senior moments'. We should be glad about all the good things we *can* remember, though. Forgetfulness can be a blessing at times. Some memories are best laid to rest. No good purpose is served by dwelling on them. I have in mind old slights and bitter grievances, for example. I remember someone saying we shouldn't nurse a grievance but should teach it to walk! The problem with some people is they forget the things they should remember and remember the things they should forget. They forget the scent of the roses and recall only the prickles!

It appears you enjoyed the blessing of being able both to remember and forget. Writing to Timothy you recalled the sincere faith which was in him and had been in his mother and grandmother before him.[1] In a similar way my heart is warmed when I recall the faith and faithfulness of dear people I've known through the years. The thought of them encourages me.

But writing to the church at Philippi you also spoke of your God-given ability to forget. You said you were forgetting what was behind and straining towards what was ahead.[2] I wonder about some of the things you felt it right to forget. Did they include persecution of Christians and the pain you caused prior to your conversion? What about the hardships you suffered in the ministry and the misunderstanding of your own Jewish people, for whom you had an undying love?

There must have been plenty of things that could have rankled in your mind and held you back as you ran the Christian race. Remembering the past could have adversely affected your future. Happily, you remembered to forget! Your own past sins were dealt with and done with, by the grace of God. The difficulties you encountered paled into insignificance as you thought about what was ahead. Your words about pressing toward the goal conjure up a picture of an athlete leaning forward, head up and straining every muscle to finish the course. They confirm for me the fact that you were a man who was able to think and act positively. You said your goal was to win the prize for which God had called you Heavenward in Christ Jesus. I can certainly relate to that.

Someone said, ironically, that his future was all behind him. But that can never be true for a Christian. We have always got something to which we can look forward, something for which to strive. Whether the past has been glorious or not, what is to come will be infinitely better. We have God's word on that. Whatever else I forget I will always remember with gratitude the wise guidance I have gained from your writings. Thank you so much.

Yours sincerely,

Wesley

¹2 Timothy 1:3-5; ²Philippians 3:13b

139

70: A letter about doubt

Dear Paul,

IN your letters you come across as a man of unshakeable faith but I wonder whether even you sometimes had to do battle with secret doubts. A man who was one of the greatest evangelists in the Church's history wrote to his hymnwriter brother in code about his secret doubts, even while he was constantly travelling and preaching his certainties. I wonder if you could relate to that. It's been said that doubt is part of being human and in today's sceptical climate it seems to be in the very air we breathe.

Doubt may arise out of intellectual considerations but I've found it helpful to weigh the alternatives to faith. I've realised that if the believer has to deal with unanswered questions the unbeliever has even more explaining to do. For example, how did a marvellously ordered universe just happen to be?

Sometimes our physical condition can give rise to doubts and I wonder whether what you called your 'thorn in the flesh' sometimes affected you spiritually. Years ago I had a serious infection and I found that doubt and depression came with the illness.

Doubt may assail us if we neglect to live close to God but did you ever find that doubt can also come despite our best efforts to live a Christian life? Some great saints who came after your time spoke of the 'dark night of the soul' when they had to hang on in blind faith, believing when they couldn't trace the way ahead. Our Lord said that even faith as small as a grain of mustard seed could work wonders and sometimes we have to fall back on the small faith we do have. For example, we believe love is better than hatred, honesty is to be preferred to deceit and so on. From such basic affirmations we may be able to move on to faith in a great God who embodies all we know to be good. Does that seem right to you?

With your grounding in religious training you may not have had the problems I have indicated. On the other hand, if you did, you quite reasonably must have felt you shouldn't disturb your converts by revealing your own private struggles. I'm sure you found in prayer, the study of Scripture and Christian fellowship the means of grace which helped build up your faith. If you had doubts you would have brought them to the Lord and urged your converts to do the same. Some of them may have echoed the words of a man who, according to your colleague Mark, came to Jesus and said: 'I do believe; help me overcome my unbelief.'[1]

I think you would agree that faith is more than feelings which may be spasmodic at times. It's a gift from God as well as the means by which we obtain more gifts from him. You wrote to your friends in Rome about 'righteousness that is by faith from first to last, just as it is written, "The righteous will live by faith."'[2] That isn't always easy but I've proved it's possible.

Yours sincerely,

Wesley

[1]Mark 9:24; [2]Romans 1:17

71: A letter about 'letters written on hearts'

Dear Paul,

SOME of my friends tease me because although I keep writing to you I get no replies. Happily, the letters you wrote long ago raise plenty of matters which prompt me to write in return. You will be astonished to know you must be the most famous writer of letters in the history of correspondence.

Letter writing is a dying art these days although there are other ways of communication which are truly wonderful. We have the means to hear people speaking to us from the other side of the world, as though they were in the next room. For example, I appreciate being able to speak with my family – including my grandchildren – thousands of miles away. Then, by electronic means we are able to exchange written messages and even see images of them instantaneously, which is marvellous. However, there's still something to be said for an old-fashioned letter which can be read and reread and preserved as an almost living link with someone. Your own letters have linked you with millions of people and have also helped to put them in touch with the Lord. That's awesome.

In addition to what you penned on papyrus there was 'writing' of a different kind. In one of your letters to the church in Corinth, you said: 'You yourselves are our letter, written on our hearts, known and read by everybody. You show that you are a letter from Christ, the result of our ministry, written not with ink but with the Spirit of the living God, not on tablets of stone but on tablets of human hearts.'[1] It seems that behind what you said was the common practice of giving people letters of commendation or what we call references. You described some of your own achievements then wondered whether what you had written sounded like self-commendation. Is that right? In fact your converts were in themselves testimony to the value of your ministry. They were all the references that could be required. Through you the Spirit of God had written his message on many hearts and the thought of that must make you 'humbly proud'.

I've found that with Christian writing it's often impossible to know all that has been accomplished. But sometimes God, for our encouragement, provides an inkling that through his Spirit the work is being blessed more than we realise. In a roundabout way I received word that a man in a distant city had found one of my books on a rubbish tip! However, he had read it and wanted me to know that his life had been turned around; the message had been inscribed on his heart. Thanks be to God!

I guess that in writing, or speaking come to that, the important thing is not what we get out of our heads but what we get into the minds of other people. If, by the grace of God, we can communicate something which will help point someone in the right direction then that will be reward in itself. I'm sure that was how you felt and it's my feeling too.

Yours sincerely,

Wesley

[1] *2 Corinthians 3:2, 3*

72: A letter about Father God

Dear Paul,

WHEN my son was born, a fellow Christian minister told me: 'You'll understand a lot more about God now you're a parent.' He was right. There have been many joys as well as a few pains of parenthood and these have brought insights with them. It's been wonderful to share in God's creativity and then see children growing up. To feel them responding in love has been reward in itself. But on occasion there has been concern as well and a desire to save children from the results of wrong decisions, without restricting their God-given gift of free will.

There's no clue that you had any physical family although some have suggested, without any hard evidence, that you may have been married at one time, which may well surprise you. Yet I think you had a father heart which contributed to your understanding of God. And wouldn't I be right in saying you were a family man in that you regarded your converts as your spiritual children?

Let me remind you, if that's necessary, of some of the things you penned. You described Christians in Galatia as 'my dear children'.[1] To people in the Church at Corinth you wrote, 'I speak as to my children.'[2] You thought of Timothy as a son.[3] I wonder, did some of your feelings as a 'father in God' help you understand more about the fatherhood of God and the joys and sorrows that could entail?

It's said that one prominent reformer in the Church found it hard to speak of God as a father because of the harshness he found in his biological father. Many of those who have unhappy home backgrounds may share that problem. Could the fact that you seem to have had no such difficulty indicate a warm relationship with your earthly father? That need not necessarily have been the case, of course.

At all events, you wrote intimately about your Heavenly Father in your letter to the Romans: 'Those who are led by the Spirit of God are sons of God. For you did not receive a spirit that makes you a slave again to fear, but you received the Spirit of sonship. And by him we cry "*Abba*, Father".'[4]

I understand that the Aramaic word *Abba* meant something like our English word 'Daddy'. To apply it to God certainly took holy boldness. Did you take a spiritual cue from our Lord himself, who used the same term when he prayed in the Garden of Gethsemene?[5] Could it be you received a first-hand report of that prayer from your associate John Mark, who may have been the mysterious young man hiding in Gethsemane, referred to in the Gospel record which bears his name?[6] Or is that no more than supposition?

At all events, like Jesus, you saw in earthly fatherhood, as it was meant to be, a reflection of the nature of God. And if God is our Heavenly Father doesn't it mean our sin is not merely an offence against an impersonal law but a blow struck at a loving heart? That seems to put a different complexion on the way we live, doesn't it?

Yours sincerely,

Wesley

[1]Galatians 4:19; [2]2 Corinthians 6:13; [3]1 Timothy 1:2;
[4]Romans 8:14, 15; [5]Mark 14:36; [6]Mark 14:51, 52

145

73: A letter about the complete work of grace

Dear Paul,

LACK of confidence is a real problem for some people. As a result, their approach to life is tentative and their potential tends to be unrealised. They lack confidence in their personal relationships, in decision making and in finding firm ground on which to build their faith or philosophy. By contrast, I sense you were a very confident person, not least in the religious convictions you held – or should I say, the convictions which held you? In a letter to Timothy you declared: 'I know whom I have believed and am convinced that he is able ...'.[1]

Some intelligentsia nowadays consider it less than intellectually respectable to be sure of anything, certainly in regard to any recognition of a Supreme Being. You knew what you were sure about: the power of God. But you were not over-confident about many other things. To know is not to claim to know all. With true humility you wrote to the Christians at Corinth: 'Now I know in part ...'.[2] Some things were veiled from your sight even as they are hidden from ours.

But, being sure about God, you were able to inspire others. You wrote to the church at Philippi: 'Being confident of this, that he who began a good work in you will carry it on to completion ...'.[3] Is it right to say you could see evidence of God working in the lives of new converts even more than they could see it in themselves? Your confidence would have increased their confidence, even as it continues to encourage ours.

I think you would hold that we don't glorify God by belittling what he has already done in our lives. Those who are redeemed should be ready to say so, gratefully. Even the smallest desire to be good is evidence of his working in us.

But for them, as for your new converts in Philippi, that should not be the end of the work of grace, just a beginning, for salvation is an ongoing experience – the work of a moment and the work of a lifetime. What God starts, he wants to complete. Correct? He is still working on us: we can be sure of that.

Physically speaking, we sometimes want medicine to relieve symptoms rather than treatment to remove the cause of the pain. Isn't it sometimes like that spiritually? We look for a little relief when God offers a radical cure. It's said the Lord is easy to please but hard to satisfy. He wants to give us the full treatment, which may be more than we want but not more than we need. He wants to do a big thing in and through us, if only we will let him.

That's what you taught. You made it clear that our need is for holiness. Nothing less. We are destined to be changed from glory to glory. A complete work of grace is what God wills for us, and with him working in us we can be confident that results will be achieved. Thank you for making that plain.

Yours sincerely,

Wesley

[1] *2 Timothy 1:12;* [2] *1 Corinthians 13:12b;* [3] *Philippians 1:6*

74: A letter about strength in weakness

Dear Paul,

IT might be imagined that, spiritually speaking, you were a very tough man – strong in faith, resolute in purpose and unbounded in courage. You might have identified with the proverb: 'The glory of young men is their strength'[1] even when you were no longer young. But you gave hints that you didn't always feel that strong. You would not have felt comfortable with a 'superman' label, for you had your 'down days' when it was difficult to keep going.

Concerning your appointment in Corinth you said: 'I came to you in weakness and fear, and with much trembling.'[2] That sounds as if you were in a bit of a mess at the time. You said: 'Who is weak and I do not feel weak?'[3] You could identify with people who were 'in the pits' as the saying goes, and, paradoxically, the fact that you didn't hide how you felt or put on a false show of strength has helped people identify with you. They could feel that you were human and, like them, liable to bleed when cut and bruise when struck. You didn't stand aloof but said: 'To the weak I became weak, to win the weak.'[4] People knew you were bone of their bone and flesh of their flesh, yet you were 'more than conqueror' through Christ. And what you could do they could do also.

You knew some people said you were 'unimpressive' appearance-wise, but that didn't hold you back. God could use you. That was all that mattered. The physical disability which seems to have bothered you, and about which you prayed a lot, was meant to keep you humble. So, too, I feel that sometimes the

148

Lord can use us best when we feel weak because then we are not full of ourselves. We need to rely on him. He who can use our strength can also use our weakness. Is that right?

The supreme example of strength in weakness is that of Jesus on the Cross. He could have called for an army of angels to rescue him from his enemies. Instead he let his enemies do their worst. But the Cross carries the message of the man who hung on it, not the message of those who put him there. Love triumphed. The victory was with vulnerability.

Of course, this flies in the face of conventional wisdom which says might is right and God is on the side of the big battalions. Apparently, the preaching about the Cross seemed silly in your day and to many people it still does. You wrote: 'For the message of the cross is foolishness to those who are perishing, but to us who are being saved it is the power of God.'[5]

You knew the apparent 'weakness' of God is stronger than human strength. His ways are higher than our ways but his ways are always best, if only we will believe it. We both know that to be the case.

Yours sincerely,

Wesley

[1]Proverbs 20:29; [2]1 Corinthians 2:3; [3]2 Corinthians 11:29; [4]1 Corinthians 9:22; [5]1 Corinthians 1:18

75: A letter about the grace of giving

Dear Paul,

OVER the centuries since your time on earth it has been customary in many countries to celebrate the birth of Jesus through what is called Christmas. There are special church services with songs about God giving his Son for the world, and in the same spirit it's common for people to give each other gifts.

In your letters you gave a lot of emphasis to the 'grace of giving'.[1] You seemed to suggest that as people learned to give they learned to live. Nowadays some seem to think it 'unspiritual' to make much mention of money in relation to the work of God but you had no scruples on that point. In fact you indicated that a person's giving of money could be evidence of spirituality rather than a denial of it, especially when the aim was to assist the poor. Human giving should be inspired by God's.

You spelt this out at some length in one of your letters to the Christians at Corinth and rounded off what you had to say with the words: 'Thanks be to God for his indescribable gift'.[2]

I understand that mental trauma or disease can render a person speechless, but so can other things. Faced with great art or beautiful scenery we may be 'lost for words'. I think you felt like that when you thought of the generous giving of some of your Christian friends. Even more, you would have known that words could never adequately describe what God had done in giving his Son. I've sometimes jolted people who have appeared somewhat cosy in a church service by wishing them an 'awe-full' Christmas,

150

then gone on to stress the importance of having a sense of awe at God's great love!

Would you agree it's easy to become blasé and lose a sense of wonderment at the thought of Almighty God being 'down to earth' in a baby born in a stable? Yet that wonder is something we need to keep fresh in our hearts, as you did, I'm sure. Christmas is sometimes described as a family festival. A lot of people make it an occasion for getting in touch with old friends, and in many homes feasting and festivity become the order of the day. I'm not sure that would be 'your thing'. There's little evidence that you engaged in much jollity or merrymaking. You seem to have been a very serious person. But I don't think you were a killjoy. I'm sure you wanted to see people happy in each other's company and would not have thought a little fun would be amiss. However, the danger is that at Christmas we can get 'wrapped in the trappings and trapped in the wrappings'. In other words, we can lose sight of what the festival is all about and forget the One whose birthday we're supposed to be celebrating.

For some people, those who have been bereaved for example, Christmas can be the loneliest time in the year but many find comfort in experiencing the abiding presence of Jesus. As some of us do our best to remind people of God's great gift, our own hearts are warmed again.

Yours sincerely,

Wesley

1 2 Corinthians 8:1-7 et al; 2 2Corinthians 9:15

76: A letter about God's ordinary people

Dear Paul,

DID you think some of the Christians in Corinth had become too self-important – 'too big for their boots' as we say today? If so, you certainly brought them down to earth by reminding them of what they had been. You wrote: 'Think of what you were when you were called. Not many of you were wise by human standards; not many were influential; not many were of noble birth.'[1]

Were not many of your converts slaves, 'non-persons' in the eyes of some? A majority came from what would now be termed the lower socio-economic strata of society. There were exceptions, like Dionysus, an influential figure in Athens, and Sergius Paulus, the proconsul who came under your ministry in Cyprus. Apollos was apparently an academic who brought his learning to the service of the gospel. Then in Corinth there may have been a sprinkling of people financially better off, like Gaius, for instance.

But would you not agree that your experience, and the history of the Church generally, is the story of God doing extraordinary things through ordinary people? Many people through the centuries have received social as well as spiritual uplift through the influence of the gospel on them or members of their family.

In your day most people were first generation Christians, but many of today's Christians have Christian forebears whose lives were changed by the gospel. For example, I know people whose grandparents were drunkards and poverty stricken because of dependence on alcohol. Then Christ brought change. Their material as well as their spiritual situation improved and their children and grandchildren have had better living standards and education as a result. But sometimes such children and grandchildren need reminding that they owe it all to Jesus. If you were around you wouldn't be slow to point that out, I'm sure.

When it comes to evangelism we sometimes find that a cultural chasm exists between those who have grown up in Christian homes and those who have not. Bridging the gap can be difficult. In some cities Christian families are less likely to live in slum areas but settle in affluent suburbs where the larger churches tend to be. This means the materially poor, who Jesus said are always with us, may be a little further away. The challenge is to move downmarket and engage in incarnational ministry, which is a big ask.

Of course, there is often spiritual need in affluent districts. There are plenty of well-dressed and educated sinners who, when it comes to moral and spiritual matters, can be incredibly foolish. Sometimes pride makes it more difficult for people like that to recognise and confess their need of a Saviour and this is a challenge for evangelists.

However, despite difficulties, I'm glad to report good success. Souls are being saved, people are being built up in the faith and new initiatives are being taken to reach out to a needy world. Thank you for the help your writings have given to those of us who seek to pursue the mission of the Lord.

Yours sincerely

Wesley

¹*1 Corinthians 1:26*

77: A letter about God's special love

Dear Paul,

I WAS brought up on the English, 'King James' translation of the Bible which now tends to be regarded as archaic although I still love its stately style. In that version a favourite text was from your letter to the Christians in Rome: 'We know that all things work together for good to them that love God, to them who are called according to his purpose.' The more modern translation I use in these letters puts it like this: 'We know that in all things God works for the good of those who love him.'[1] Does that better express what you had in mind? It probably does.

You made clear that a qualifying factor is 'to those who love God'. But how on earth is it possible to love someone we've never seen? Would you agree that the answer may be that first we should love those qualities which Scripture tells us are characteristic of God: love, faithfulness, holiness and so on?

However, in all honesty, it may be hard to love abstractions. I have heard tell of people 'in love with love' but most of us want to see fine qualities personified – virtue in a skin, integrity lived out, love in action. Isn't that why the Word became flesh, as your colleague the Apostle John put it? Didn't Jesus come to be the human focus of the nature of God, an Ideal who was also bone of our bone and flesh of our flesh? That's my reading of the many inspired words you had to say on the subject. We love God because he first loved us.[2] It's his love which evokes a response in us.

Of course, the love that God revealed in Christ and the Holy Spirit inspires in us is not just any sort of love. I understand that the special word for this special kind of love was the Greek *agape* which you saw as the key to a right relationship with God, and victorious living.

In your letter to the Romans you catalogued some of the things which might have been thought capable of separating people from the love of Christ. Among those things were persecution, famine, nakedness or danger – things which you had undergone yourself. But you could testify: 'In all these things we are more than conquerors through him who loved us.'[3] Your faith had been tried in the fires of adversity and was stronger as a result. You never suggested that Christianity would bring exemption from troubles. It is no cheap insurance policy. Sometimes it leads to additional challenges. Christ didn't come to make life easy but to make victorious living possible. We were not meant merely to survive but to thrive; not just to get by but to be 'more than conquerors'.

It's been suggested that when you wrote those words the picture in your mind was of a Roman general returning to base victorious after an overwhelmingly successful campaign. Was that the case? At all events, at the end of your life when for you a condemned cell was really God's waiting room, you could say: 'I have fought the good fight, I have finished the race, I have kept the faith.'[4] I'm sure your words didn't indicate self-congratulation but gratitude for grace.

Yours sincerely,

Wesley

[1]*Romans 8:28;* [2]*Romans 5:5, 8;* [3]*Romans 8:37;* [4]*2 Timothy 4:7*

78: A letter about God's special days

Dear Paul,

I FIND time seems to pass more quickly as I get older. Days, weeks and months fly by. It's been wryly remarked that when we are over the hill the pace seems faster! For some a new year may be a time for feasting and festivity but for those of us who are Christians it is an occasion for reflection, gratitude and rededication.

You may know that in a large part of the world the calendar takes the birth of Jesus Christ as a fixed point with dates designated BC (before Christ) and AD (meaning *anno domini* 'in the year of our Lord') for time subsequent to his coming. Don't you think it great that many unbelievers as well as believers take account of *our* Jesus every time they date their letters? It's just one of the ways in which people recognise the mark he has made upon history.

I'm sure you would agree that the coming of Jesus represents much more than a date on the calendar. Every year can properly be seen as a 'year of grace' and although the lordship of Christ is still not universally accepted he reigns in the hearts of many of us. And one day, as you anticipated, *every* knee will bow at his name and every tongue confess that he is Lord.[1]

In many churches the coming of a new year is marked by 'watchnight' services when people repent of past failures and resolve to do better in the future, with God's help. But there are other times also when our lives need to be punctuated and our living re-enlivened by grace. As a long sentence sags without punctuation, so our lives need days of dedication and times of renewal. In your Jewish religion you may have found life rather flat without high days and holidays. Certainly the early Christian Church instituted special times designed to maintain the faithful in their devotional life.

You wrote to friends in Rome: 'I urge you ... in view of God's mercy, to offer your bodies as living sacrifices, holy and pleasing to God – this is your spiritual act of worship.'[2] For that, there's no time like the present.

Yours sincerely,

Wesley

[1]*Philippians 2:10, 11;* [2]*Romans 12:1*

79: And finally!

Dear Paul,

I SMILED when I heard of some church choirboys who said when the preacher said 'lastly' he often lasted a lot longer! With respect, I've noticed that, in your letters, after you said 'finally' you sometimes had quite a few more things to add. I'm glad you did, for some of those additions are very important.

To the Church at Ephesus you said: 'Finally, be strong in the Lord and in his mighty power.'[1] That's an encouragement which helps us to brace up when we might wilt and weaken. Our battle may be fierce but good soldiers are meant to be tough – not spiritual wimps. As you said to Timothy, we have to endure hardness.

Writing to the Philippian Christians your words were: 'Finally ... rejoice in the Lord!'[2] You wanted your people to be happy warriors not just dutiful in a dour sort of way. Is that right? Some people seem to have only enough religion to make them miserable! I'm glad I have enough to make me happy, and I think you would say the same.

To the same people you wrote: 'Finally ... whatever is true, whatever is noble ... think about such things.'[3] You knew the biggest battles are often within our own minds. That's where the holy war is won or lost. The assault on our souls is continuous and the threat of invasion comes through our thinking. Therefore your warning is still timely. To be forewarned is to be forearmed.

To the Thessalonians you said: 'Finally ... pray for us that the message of the Lord may spread rapidly.'[4] Am I right in thinking you had in mind the progress of Greek runners speeding with

158

important messages? It seems like that. You asked people to pray for you. Would you still make that request? Do you still need prayer? Or is it no longer called for? The Church has often spoken of the communion of saints, including those in Heaven, and when I read your words I frequently feel my heart beating in time with yours. Here, we mortals are in the realm of mystery.

To your people at Corinth you wrote: 'Finally ... goodbye.'[5] I have a feeling that, for you as for me, farewells may sometimes have been difficult. Paradoxically, we are sometimes sorry to leave and also glad to go. We may be saddened at the thought of not seeing well-loved faces again yet cheered at the prospect of making new friends.

Of course, for those of us with faith no parting need be finally final. As it has been said: 'With God every apparent end is only a more glorious new beginning.' The good life in Christ we have known is to be continued. You certainly believed that and now, I am sure, you have proved it to be true. I'm confident that God is blessing you beyond anything I can imagine.

Yours sincerely,

Wesley

[1]*Ephesians 6:10;* [2]*Philippians 3:1;* [3]*Philippians 4:8;*
[4]*2 Thessalonians 3:1;* [5]*2 Corinthians 13:11*

159